The Death of Captain Cook

ONE WEEK LOAN

Renew Books on PHONE-it: 01443 654456

Books are to be returned on or before the last date below

Title-page, 'Some Account of a Voyage to South Seas in 1776–1777–1778', with a silhouette of David Samwell in uniform. British Library, London, Egerton MS 2591 fo.1 6/7157.

THE DEATH OF CAPTAIN COOK

AND OTHER WRITINGS

BY

DAVID SAMWELL

Edited by
Martin Fitzpatrick, Nicholas Thomas and Jennifer Newell

UNIVERSITY OF WALES PRESS
CARDIFF
2007

British Library Cataloguing in Publication Data
A catalogue record for this book is available from the British Library.

ISBN 978-0-7083-2073-0 paperback
ISBN 978-0-7083-1968-0 hardback

Printed in Great Britain by Antony Rowe Ltd, Wiltshire

for Iain McCalman

Contents

Illustrations

Preface

This book republishes a classic of Pacific exploration. *A Narrative of the Death of Captain James Cook, to which are added some particulars concerning his life and character, and observations respecting the introduction of the venereal disease into the Sandwich Islands*, which first appeared in 1786, provided a searching and extended account of what was, from the European point of view, one of the most dramatic and tragic episodes in the history of the Pacific. Its author, David Samwell, was a surgeon, voyager, poet, antiquarian and radical. As we explain in the introductory chapters that follow, Samwell's account of Cook's end was substantially incorporated into the first full biography of the navigator, published by Andrew Kippis in 1788 and widely translated, reprinted and rehashed, not only during the epoch, but throughout the nineteenth century and into the twentieth. Samwell's perspective upon an event that has been extensively debated for more than two hundred years was therefore profoundly if indirectly influential, but Samwell's original pamphlet has been reprinted only twice (in 1916 and 1957) in limited editions; both these and the original are scarce items even in research libraries.

This edition aims, in addition to making a fascinating and important work accessible, to publish a wider range of relevant material that enables an understanding of the personal background and preoccupations that made Samwell, like the naturalists on Cook's first and second voyages, Joseph Banks, Johann Reinhold and Georg Forster, an entertaining, distinctive and imaginative commentator on a rich and varied voyage of foundational importance in the histories of European exploration and colonial contact in the Pacific. A lively series of letters from Samwell to the Liverpool merchant Matthew Gregson is extant; a few of these were cited and quoted by Cook's editor and biographer, J. C. Beaglehole, in *The Journals of Captain James Cook*, but they have not generally been drawn upon by those debating Cook's third voyage and his death. Here, all the letters concerned with the period and experiences of the expedition are published for the first time, together with relevant extracts from others. To give readers a fuller sense of Samwell as a writer and cultural figure, we also republish a number of Samwell's poems that illuminate his attitudes to race, slavery, voyaging and Welsh tradition.

Acknowledgements

Martin Fitzpatrick wishes to thank the Centre for Cross-Cultural Research at the Australian National University for a fellowship in 1998, Tsari Anderson for her research assistance in Canberra, Dawn Cross for her assistance in transcribing the Samwell–Gregson Correspondence, Geraint Lewis for his translation of Samwell's St David's Day poem, Ffion Mair Jones and David Ceri Jones for sharing information on Samwell, and Daniel Huws and Geraint Phillips for their invaluable expert advice. The editors also thank Herb Kane for his comments on a draft of this edition, the Centre for Cross-Cultural Research for funding the scanning of Samwell's text, and the Liverpool Record Office, Liverpool Libraries and Information Services for permission to publish the relevant parts of the correspondence. Iain McCalman initiated this edition with Nicholas Thomas in 1997. Though other commitments required him to withdraw from a co-editorial role, his radical re-imagining of the Romantic period has been fundamental to our approach to this book. But in addition to this intellectual stimulation, we also thank him for his unfailing support and friendship.

MHF, NT, JN
October 2006

Introduction

When David Samwell was born in 1751 Britain was already well on the way to becoming a great power. The foundations for such status were laid by the Glorious Revolution of 1688–9. It ensured that Britain would be governed by a Protestant monarch, soon by a German dynasty, and by permanent representative Parliamentary institutions, which set limits on the king's authority and guaranteed, in Voltaire's optimistic view, that 'the prince is all powerful to do good, and at the same time is restrained from committing evil'.[1] Under William III, Britain inherited the mantle of the Dutch as the leader of a coalition of powers, which sought to check the ambitions of Louis XIV of France. In 1694 the Bank of England was founded, which placed the war effort on a sound financial footing and assisted the development of English commerce. The Scots attempted to follow suit, but failed. The union with England in 1707 was the price they paid to participate in the English financial revolution and commercial prosperity. United, Britain became a formidable European power, defeating the France of both Louis XIV and Louis XV. By 1763, with the Peace of Paris which ended the Seven Years War, Britain had defeated the French not only in Europe and on the high seas, but in India and North America. Around the same time (1760), a new young monarch, George III, had ascended the throne. Although a Hanoverian, he had been brought up in England. Great hopes rested on his shoulders. Britain would demonstrate to the rest of Europe true enlightened government and kingship.

Ever since the Glorious Revolution, the British had believed that they were leading exemplars of a new form of revolution: an intellectual revolution, which would apply new knowledge to all aspects of life. In an oft-quoted euphoric utterance, the third Earl of Shaftesbury, who had been tutored by the philosopher John Locke, declared, 'there is a mighty light which spreads over the world, especially in those two free nations England and Holland, on whom the affairs of all Europe now turn'.[2] By 1763 the affairs had clearly turned in favour of the free nations, and the scene was set for enlightenment to spread beyond Europe. George III, indeed, took a keen interest in voyages of enlightened discovery. He was an enthusiastic

amateur astronomer and would later assist William Herschel with funds
for constructing his reflective telescopes, which enabled him to discover
the planet Uranus (1781), and begin the classification of nebulae. In 1782
Herschel was appointed Astronomer Royal. George III also ensured that
John Harrison was paid the balance of the prize offered by the Board of
Longitude for calculating longitude accurately at sea. Harrison had
developed a reliable maritime chronometer for the purpose. When Cook
took a copy of Harrison's chronometer on his second expedition, it lost
barely two minutes a year. The board had been reluctant to pay Harrison all
the prize money of £20,000. George III put that right.[3] He also supported
Captain James Cook's first expedition to the Pacific, which had the scientific task of witnessing from Tahiti the transit of Venus in order to assist in
measuring the distance between the earth and the sun, and the earth and
Venus. The king gave the Royal Society £4,000 to cover the cost of sending
observers.[4] His interest in voyaging did not stop there. His mother had
founded the Royal Botanical Gardens at Kew in 1759, and the king was
keen to know about the new botanical knowledge which the voyages
would bring. Indeed, in his preface to his account of Cook's voyage, John
Hawkesworth suggested that George III had helped to inaugurate a whole
new era of enlightened imperialism, in which the objectives were the
pursuit and diffusion of knowledge and the development of commerce,
rather than conquest and exploitation. More had been achieved in the seven
years of voyaging climaxed by Cook's first expedition than in the whole
period since Columbus had discovered America![5] George III never ceased
to be interested in Cook's voyaging. When Samwell sailed on the third
voyage, the *Resolution* and the *Discovery* carried on board animals which
the king had donated from the royal farms, 'with a view', as George III himself put it, 'of stocking Otaheite and the neighbouring islands with these
useful animals'.[6] By 1788, when Revd Andrew Kippis published his biography of Cook – mainly a compilation of voyage accounts, which remained
the standard account for over a century – the idea that the voyages were part
of a wider Enlightenment enterprise became set in stone. Like Hawkesworth,
he gave George III special credit: 'Without your Majesty's munificence and
encouragement the world would have remained destitute of that immense
light which has been thrown on geography, navigation, and the most important sciences.'[7] Such claims were part of an attempt to make sense of
Britain's new-found power and influence, and must not be taken at face-
value. In the very same dedication Kippis, a Rational Dissenting minister,
expressed the devout wish 'that the virtue of this country were equal to
its knowledge'. Indeed, the hopes that the nation would have a patriotic
monarch who was above politics, providing a focus for a harmonious, united,
imperial Britain, had already been dashed – at home by the fragmentation

of party politics and fears about the influence of George's Scottish tutor, John Stuart, third earl of Bute, and abroad by the new assertiveness of the colonies in North America, which were no longer constrained by fear of French power on their continent. Patriotic aspirations were, however, never realistic, and were unlikely to have been realized, even had the colonial tensions and party strife been handled more effectively. Britain in the late eighteenth century contributed to and was affected by trends which affected the whole western world. The American colonists in their successful struggle with Britain boldly asserted their right to life, liberty and happiness. At home the period would witness campaigns for parliamentary reform, religious reform and greater toleration for dissenters, and for the abolition of the slave trade. The language of such campaigners was usually that of universal rights, that is, of the rights of individuals to live freely and to shape their own future, but often those involved were seeking the rights of particular communities. The historian of these changes, R. R. Palmer, has portrayed the conflicts and upheavals of the time as crises of community. He has drawn attention to the way in which groups that had once felt themselves to be part of a community suddenly felt left out, and other groups previously regarded as of no political significance and of low social standing began to assert themselves, and demand participation and integration. In this process, new questions were asked about the nature of politics and society and the overall identity of communities.

Communal or collective identity is rarely simple. Linda Colley has reminded us that at least until the end of the nineteenth century 'the majority of people in the British Isles were never possessed by an overwhelming and exclusive sense of their own distinctive identity as Englishmen, as Scotsmen, Welshmen or even as Irishmen'.[8] Nonetheless, even as the new identity of Britain and Britishness was being shaped in the eighteenth century, the process of unification led to a re-examination of the identity of the peripheral nations and the communities within them, the Welsh, the Scots and the Irish, as well as to some tentative steps towards the understanding of Englishness. No sooner had Britannia ruled the waves in the wars of the mid-century, than self-doubt set in, not least as a result of the American challenge. Some of the questions posed were about the nature of the constitution. Were the rights enjoyed by Britons ancient rights or were they abstract universal rights enjoyed by all of humanity? And, if these rights were universal, were they not also natural, enjoyed by men in a state of nature? The answer to such questions could be sought by studying more 'savage' societies and by studying the ancient past.

No one doubted that being a Briton was virtuous, but who were the authentic Britons? Were they Celts or Anglo-Saxons, Scottish, Welsh or English? Within the broad concept of Britishness, the nations and communities within Britain examined their histories in the quest for the authentic, aboriginal Britons. A complex process was under-way, in which Britishness was confidently asserted to the outside world, particularly later in the century when the wars with revolutionary France began, whilst within Britain historians and antiquarians engaged in a scramble for their nation's histories, which they pursued to the very brink of historical time. They may have been only an educated minority, but they would play a crucial role in shaping the sense of nationhood for their contemporaries and for the future.

Placed in this broad context, the voyages of discovery as manifestations of enlightened imperialism and of the great appetite to know more about aboriginal peoples make more sense. This is not to suggest that easy generalizations can be made about how the search for identity at home affected encounters in the far-away Pacific and how those encounters affected concerns about identity at home. Dissecting a symbiotic relationship can be difficult, especially when the materials for understanding that relationship are relatively limited. For the most part the journals and recollections of the encounters were written by those of whom we know very little, and certainly not enough to locate them with any detail or precision within the cultural politics of Britain. This is, of course, not true of some of the major players, British or otherwise, such as the naturalist Sir Joseph Banks, subsequently long-serving President of the Royal Society and effectually curator of Kew Gardens, or the Swedish botanist Daniel Solander, both leading lights of the first expedition (1768–71), or the German father-and-son duo of Johann Reinhold and George Forster, who left distinguished accounts of the second expedition (1772–75). For them, it is possible to reconstruct their cultural identities. It is rarely possible to do the same for lesser participants. Fortunately, that is not the case with David Samwell, one of the liveliest memorialists of Pacific encounters and one who was deeply interested in the issues of the day. The painstaking work of William Llewellyn Davies in the 1920s and 1930s revealed a good deal about Samwell's life and thought. [9] He had read Samwell's journal of Cook's third expedition (1776–79), but its contents were not more generally available until J. L. Beaglehole published the journals of Cook's third expedition, in 1967. [10] In his magisterial *Life of Captain James Cook*, Beaglehole describes Samwell as 'highly Welsh', and his journal as conveying, 'as did no other . . . the more frivolous side of a voyage that had its frivolities as well as its moments of tragedy'. [11] More recently, O. H. K. Spate has portrayed Samwell as the 'rollicking Welsh surgeon'. [12] There is no doubt that Samwell intended his journal to be entertaining, that his blood was easily warmed by native women willing to exchange sexual favours, and that he was a passionate Welsh bard. Yet there is a danger in such characterizations of creating a caricatural view of the writer and of his journal, Samwell's account becoming the 'boyo' version of cultural exchange. Given the theatricality of encounters,[13] the apparently frivolous requires serious consideration, and the perceptions of Samwell, who undoubtedly, as Spate notes, was a 'completely participant' observer will repay close study.[14] Samwell, moreover, was a complex and multi-talented character, and in what follows we move beyond facile characterizations and explore the many facets of the man. Some of the material which we are publishing is new, some is made accessible for the first time. Samwell's correspondence with Matthew Gregson was consulted by Beaglehole for his study of Cook, but it naturally played a minor role. His work was consulted by E. G. Bowen for his excellent short bilingual study of Samwell, but he did not follow up the references to the Samwell–Gregson correspondence.[15] We publish in full Samwell's letters from that correspondence relating to Cook's third voyage and its immediate aftermath, and extracts concerning the voyages from later correspondence.[16] In the first two chapters we use that correspondence generally and extensively to enable us to make new connections between the various worlds Samwell inhabited and the cultures in which he participated. This is followed by an evaluation of Samwell's account of the death of Captain Cook and of his observations on indigenous societies. It is hoped that our studies of the contexts of his life and thought reveal in a new way the nature of his priorities and pre-conceptions, and will lead to a fuller understanding of his encounters in the Pacific.

Notes

[1]   Letters Concerning the English Nation (1733), in Christopher Thacker (ed.), *Voltaire: Selected Writings* (London: Everyman, 1995), Letter VIII, p. 31.

[2]   Peter Gay, *The Enlightenment: An Interpretation: The Rise of Modern Paganism* (London: Weidenfeld & Nicolson, 1967), p. 11.

[3]   Alan Villiers, *Captain Cook: The Seamen's Seaman* (Harmondsworth: Penguin Books, 2001 [London, 1967]), pp. 86, 154, 193; the copy of the chronometer was made by a Mr Kendal and was known as 'Kendal's watch'.

[4]   Christopher Hibbert, *George III: A Personal History* (Harmondsworth: Penguin Books, 1999), p. 195 n.*.

[5]   John Hawkesworth, *An Account of the Voyages, Undertaken by Order of His Present Majesty for making Discoveries in the Southern Hemisphere: by Commodore Byron, Captain Wallis, Captain Carteret, and Captain Cook, in the Dolphin, Swallow and Endeavour . . .* , 3 vols (London: Strahan and Cadell, 1773), I, Dedication To the King, 1 May 1773. It is important to note that the development of commerce was seen not as exploitation but as a key aspect of communication between peoples, and often as part of a providential design for the improvement of

mankind. See Richard Price, 'The Evidence for a Future Period of Improvement in the State of Mankind' (1787) in D. O. Thomas (ed.), *Richard Price: Political Writings* (Cambridge: Cambridge University Press, 1991), pp. 152–75 (p. 162).

6   Richard Hough, *Captain James Cook: A Biography* (London: Hodder and Stoughton, 1994), p. 341. See also Hibbert, *George III*, pp. 193–7 for George's interest in science, instrument-making and farming.

7   A. Kippis, *A Narrative of the Voyages Round the World Performed by Captain James Cook . . .* (London: Bickers and Son, 1893), p. v, dedication to first edition, 13 June 1788.

8   Linda Colley, 'Britishness and Otherness: an Argument', in Michael O'Dea and Kevin Welan (eds), *Nations and Nationalisms: France, Britain, Ireland and the Eighteenth-Century Context* (Oxford: Voltaire Foundation, 1995), Studies on Voltaire and the Eighteenth Century, 335, pp. 61–77 (p. 65).

9   W. L .Davies, 'David Samwell (1751–1798)', *Transactions of the Honourable Society of Cymmrodorion*, 1926–7, 70–133; 'David Samwell: A Further Note,' *Transactions of the Honourable Society of Cymmrodorion*, 1937–8, 257–8; 'David Samwell's Poem – "The Padouca Hunt"', *The National Library of Wales Journal*, II, 1941–2, 142–52.

10 Beaglehole, *The Journals of Captain James Cook* (Cambridge: Hakluyt Society, 1955–67), III [hereafter Beaglehole, *Journals*], pp. 989–1300.

11 Beaglehole, *The Life of Captain James Cook* (Cambridge: Hakluyt Society, 1974 [initially pub. as vol. IV of Beaglehole, *Journals,* but repr. separately by A. & C. Black, London, and by Stanford University Press]), p. 500.

12 O. H. K. Spate, *The Pacific since Magellan*, vol. III, *Paradise Found and Lost* (London: Routledge, 1988), p. 238.

13 Greg Dening, 'The Theatricality of Observing and being Observed: Eighteenth-century Europe "discovers" the ? century "Pacific"', in Stuart B. Schwartz (ed.), *Implicit Understandings: Observing, Reporting, and Reflecting on the Encounters between Europeans and Other Peoples in the Early Modern Era* (Cambridge, New York: Cambridge University Press, 1994), pp. 451–82 (p.453).

14 Spate, *The Pacific since Magellan*, p.238.

15 E. G. Bowen, *David Samwell (Dafydd Ddu Feddyg) 1751–1798* (Caerdydd: Gwasg Prifysgol Cymru, 1974).

16 J. C. Beaglehole published extracts from the correspondence in Appendix V, 'Calendar of documents', leaving out 'badinage' and other things he considered irrelevant. *Journals*, pp. 1481–565.

'David Samwell', engraving by Chrétien after Fouqueh, Paris, 1798. Formerly in
the possession of Matthew Gregson. British Library, London,
Egerton MS 2591 fo.2 7951129.

1

David Samwell: an eventful career

MARTIN FITZPATRICK

David Samwell was born on 15 October 1751. His father, William Samuel, was vicar of Nantglyn, near Denbigh, in north Wales. It was a cultured family. Samwell's grandfather, Revd Edward Samuel of Llangar, was a learned man, a poet and translator into Welsh of major works of Christian literature. Samwell grew up with a love of poetry and a sense of the power of inherited tradition. He was fascinated by old manuscripts and ancient artefacts. Throughout his life he enjoyed visiting historic sites and seeking out locals with memories of past events. The young Samwell was a bright lad and was sent to one of the local grammar schools, probably Ruthin. Dr Johnson defined a grammar school as 'a school in which the learned languages are grammatically taught'.[1] Samwell was taught by such standards, imbibing a love of Latin literature. On his voyage with Captain Cook, he would take his school textbook of the works of his favourite Latin poet, Horace.[2] Unlike several of his friends in later life, he was not self-taught, for he received an education which would have been a fit preparation for university, had his parents had the wherewithal to send him. But the Welsh clergy were poorly paid; the episcopate was English in complexion, and the richer livings were distributed amongst English clerics. After leaving grammar school Samwell would have to shift for himself.

Welsh was the language of Samwell's hearth and home, but it was not the language of his grammar schooling. The Act of Union of 1536 ensured that English (and Latin) was the language of the administration. Its potentially disastrous impact on the Welsh language was mitigated by Elizabethan legislation, which ensured that Welsh would be the language of the established Church, and by the translation of the Bible into Welsh. However, when grammar schools were set up in Wales in the sixteenth and seventeenth centuries they taught through the medium of English. They were designed for Welshmen who wanted to get on in the world, and Welsh literacy was not a requirement for such aspirants. There were undoubtedly some informal exceptions to the anti-Welsh rule, and some masters at Ruthin may have taught in Welsh.[3] Nonetheless, education was predominantly in English. Samwell was not someone to harbour grievances, but later in life he did regret that he was not as literate in Welsh as in English. On 6 July 1793, he wrote to his friend Walter Davies, 'I wish I could write Welsh as fluent as you, then I might make my correspondence much more agreeable to the Nant [Thomas Edwards] than I can at present.'[4]

   The limited resources of Samwell's family meant that he was dependent on his wits for his success. The death of his only brother in 1772 did not alter the situation. A few years later, at a trough in his development, he confessed to his friend Matthew Gregson that his only expectation from his family was when he received his 'portion', that is, when his father died. When that happened, in the 1790s, he was bequeathed a small patch of land which, he wrote, yielded an annual rent of £10 – and the tenant jibbed at that. By then, fortunately he had a secure income. In 1774, he contemplated serving on the slave-traders – the 'guinea ships' – but managed to avoid this odious employment. In October the following year he gained his certificate as second mate, third rate, before the Court of Examiners of the Royal College of Surgeons. He was now qualified to rise to the rank of surgeon. Samwell had been apprenticed to the naval surgeon, John Crosier, who proved to be a good friend and patron. Crosier had sailed with John Byron on an expedition of exploration in the South Atlantic and the Pacific. Amongst its objectives was to discover a north-west passage – one of the aims of Cook's third expedition. The expedition was a modest success, and it was immediately followed by a further expedition by Wallis and Carteret.[5] Their ships became separated and their voyages continued independently. Both had their successes, the most notable being Wallis's discovery of Tahiti. Samwell would learn all about these in due course.

   Byron and his crew on the *Dolphin* returned to England in May 1766. Samwell could have become apprenticed to John Crosier any time after that. We know very little about his whereabouts over the next decade. His base generally was in London where he lived with Crosier, but early on in this period he got to know Matthew Gregson. Indeed, it seems likely that he first travelled to Liverpool to seek his fortune. A rapidly growing seaport adjacent to North Wales, it was a natural first port-of-call for an ambitious lad from Denbigh.[6] We know that Samwell was in Liverpool for the election of Richard Pennant. This could have been in either the autumn of 1767 or the spring of 1768.[7] Pennant was of Welsh ancestry, his family belonging to a collateral line of descent to that of Thomas Pennant, a distinguished travel-writer, antiquarian and natural historian, and a leading figure in the Welsh Enlightenment. Richard was also, by inheritance through his mother's side, a wealthy Jamaican landowner and therefore slave-owner.[8] However, he had Samwell's boisterous support. Recalling that time seven years on, he wrote to Gregson:

denyed through the influence of malign Stars for these 7 years past, one glorious golden opportunity of distinguishing my zeal in the cause [of Patriotism] by demolishing the Lamps & Windows of the ungodly – No, never since the Liverpool Election, have I had an opportunity of serving my Country, when I gave undoubted proofs of my future greatness by making a lamp tumble before me & half a dozen windows rattle to the tune of Pennant for ever.[9]

Pennant was a Whig and was supported by – or paid for the support of – the Greenland fishermen. They had their own ways of intimidating the opposition with the blubber knives used for cutting up whales. Samwell knew these sailors, for he spent some time amongst them in the period before he sailed with Cook.[10] On one occasion he left his ship at Liverpool and travelled to London, leaving his 'whole Greenland wardrobe' behind.[11] Matthew Gregson kindly sent it on for him.

We don't know when Samwell first met Gregson, although no doubt it was sometime in the mid 1760s, when Samwell was in Liverpool. The first extant letter in their correspondence is from June 1772, but it was undoubtedly not the first letter between the two. The correspondence as it survives is entirely one-sided; that is, all the letters are to Matthew Gregson, mostly from Samwell. Nonetheless, it tells us much about Gregson, his family and his friends. He was the son of a Liverpool merchant. Although not as well-educated as Samwell – he had not been to a grammar school – he was assiduous in his self-education. Like Samwell, he was a high-spirited youth, a lover of art and poetry, and of antiquities. Both admired the opposite sex inordinately. In politics, he was a ministerialist, supporting the administration of Lord North. Later, following the Fox–North Coalition, he supported the Whig opposition. Starting off as more conservative in politics than Samwell, he ended up as more consistently liberal. He outlived his friend by many years, and in his later life he had the distinction of refusing a knighthood from the Prince Regent for his achievements as an antiquarian. Sometime after that, the Revd Joseph Hunter F. S. A. dined with him. He left many pen-portraits of contemporaries of note; that of Gregson is not flattering: 'he seemed to me a thoroughly ignorant fellow, with some antiquarian enthusiasm. He is a shambling [?] kind of man.'[12]

One suspects that this is an educated man of one generation maligning the achievements of a self-educated man of a previous one. Maybe, too, Gregson lacked the polish required in the age of Beau Brummell. The late eighteenth-century Enlightenment in England was noted for its plain-speaking variant of candour. Yet within that fold Gregson belonged to the artistic and literary wing which was affected by sensibility. He might not meet nineteenth-century standards of polish and competence, but in his correspondence he was rather more discreet than Samwell. Particularly when it came to sex, he dressed his questions in polite euphemisms. This only goaded Samwell into responding with the crude vigour of a young libertine, especially as he knew his friend had similar inclinations. When Gregson wondered whether his friend was unwell or had met with some misfortune, as he had not heard from him for some time, he met with a characteristically exuberant response:

Hem! Hem! Hem!

In the first Epistle (since the 24th day of Feb.y 1773) of Samuel to Matthew & at the 2nd Verse, if you are not blind, you may read these Words,

'And it came to pass that Samuel said unto Matthew, of a Truth I perceive that thou art a queer Dog and no Philosopher'. . .

1st. Why then shou'd you attribute my neglect of writing to sickness or want of health, or on the other hand to misfortune or bad luck? 2ndly Because you are queer Dog and no Philosopher, & for as much as you cannot 'purtend to know life.' For so as how as it you had been anything of a Philosopher & had begun a descanting ranting or writing upon the wonderful operations of Nature, you cou'd not but have perceived or seen known or understood that my negligence had proceeded or sprung from causes or cases quite the reverse, for men are never more apt to apply to their friends than when in trouble & distress. Witness the Arch Patriot's supplication to his Majesty when under confinement in the Kings Bench – But on the contrary a sound body free from the Taint Venereal, a few pieces of a lovely, whiteness jingling heavenly Musick in the grass green purse; where with to swagger amongst the Nymphs & Goddesses in the Paradasiacal Gardens about London an Intoxication that from the giddy Heads of Youth after make them grow forgetful at their distant Friends & acquaintance Yet if I forget thee amongst ten thousand Maccaronies, if I do not remember thee in my mirth at the Pantheon may my right Hand forget it's [cunning] of making Pills, yea if I don't prefer thy health over a mug of Cambriern Ale at Merlin's Cave, may I grow so foolish as to take Pills myself; which that I may not, the Lord of his infinite Mercies grant & c.

Amen . . .

                                                            June 24th 1773.

Samwell never married, but he did develop a strong attachment sometime before he left on the third expedition. [13] Probably the only real love of his life, she died in childbirth, as did the child, while he was away, causing Samwell considerable grief. [14] Yet it is unlikely that he would have changed his ways. He was sexually lax: he loved the 'nymphs' and paid for their favours. Gregson enjoyed hearing about the exploits of his friend and, in due course, he would be anxious to know how he had fared with the maidens of the South Seas. He was less frank with Samwell about his own amours, despite frequent requests for information from his friend.

When Gregson's first wife died, he asked Samwell for some affecting lines for her headstone; Samwell obliged but was unsure of her Christian name. He thought it was Mary, and designed a line in which alternative two-syllable names would fit. Unfortunately, it was Jane.[15] Although Gregson's wife died prematurely, the fact that Samwell did not know her name is a sign that Samwell's contacts with his friend by this time were almost exclusively epistolary. In the 1780s Gregson came to London on a number of occasions but was so busy that he failed to visit Samwell. By this time, Gregson was a wealthy and established businessman. Samwell had sensed early on that he would be astute in developing his career, just as he sensed that he himself would not. In fact, Gregson briefly in the mid 1770s betrayed some uncertainty, thinking, perhaps influenced by Samwell's example, of going in for medicine.[16] Around that time he was becoming committed to the upholstery trade and so some doubts would not be surprising.[17] They were soon allayed, for Liverpool was an expanding port, growing rich and prosperous. Merchants were building themselves opulent new dwelling places, and there was a healthy demand for furnishings. In the 1780s we find Gregson was investing in the Greenland trade, and probably, given the way he defended it, the slave trade, an issue on which he was at odds with his friend. He was making enough money to be thinking of his role as a citizen and of the future of his town. Together with his friend William Roscoe, he would play a leading role in developing civic institutions appropriate to the burgeoning port.

Both Samwell and Gregson went through difficult periods in their career in the mid 1770s, and both came through them well. In Samwell's case the critical influence was John Crosier. Through him Samwell learnt about the South Seas. Crosier, as noted, was surgeon on Byron's ship, the *Dolphin*, during the circumnavigation of 1764–66. In the course of the voyage, when they were off the island of Masafuera, Byron reorganized the command of his ships, bringing Captain Mouat and his first lieutenant Philip Carteret to the *Dolphin* and sending his own first lieutenant, James Cumming, to captain the *Tamar*.[18] Carteret and Crosier became great friends and would later reminisce about the voyage and Carteret's subsequent exploits in the Pacific in the *Swallow*. As soon as Hawkesworth's account of their voyages and of Cook's first voyage was published Samwell had obtained a copy and was writing of his interests to Gregson:

> There is lately published an Account of the 3 voyages made around the world by the Dolphin, Swallow & Endeavour.[19] Mr Crosier was in the Dolphin & Capt.n Carteret [20] of the Swallow was twice round the World, the first time he was Lieutenant of the Dolphin & afterwards in the Swallow, he often dines with his old shipmate Mr Crosier, I have read the first volume which gives an account of many Nations never heard of before & of many surprizing Adventures which one reads with double the Pleasure as being acquainted with some of the Adventurers & having heard some of the circumstances mentioned by those concerned in them before they were published.[21]

Gregson, encouraged by Samwell to read Hawkesworth, offered some comments of his own, which Samwell told him were 'ingenious and worthy of yourself'. This occurred in a long and effervescent letter, and Samwell did not pause to comment further;[22] a pity, for Samwell would have been well aware of the controversy over the book, which Fanny Burney believed hastened Hawkesworth's death.[23] More particularly, it is likely that he would have known of Carteret's criticisms of the way Hawkesworth had used his journal. He would have heard at first hand Crosier's opinions of his treatment of Byron's voyage, including his amplification of comments on the physique of the Patagonians so that they appeared as veritable giants and the voyagers as pygmies. Wallis and Carteret both took careful note of the size of the Patagonians, on their subsequent voyage and came back with much more sober estimates of their size. Hawkesworth, however, erred on the side of exaggeration rather than caution.[24] Samwell, who liked a good argument, would have had his imagination stimulated by their discussions.[25] Both he and Gregson loved to delve into the past. In 1770 Samwell had been one of the first members of the Gwyneddigion Society which, formed from Welshmen from Gwynedd (North Wales), was intended to stimulate interest in Welsh literary and musical traditions.[26] In hearing and reading of the South Seas, he would not only be fascinated by accounts of a quite different world – of man-eating sharks, of Kangaroos, of exotic landscapes and of beautiful women without sexual inhibitions – but in thinking of such an 'other' he would be aware of the 'other' British and European pasts which so fascinated him. He would find that the illustrations in Hawkesworth also made connections between Europe's past and the native civilizations, for the natives sometimes were decked in what might be interpreted as Roman togas.[27] In the circumstances, reading Horace in the South Seas might be regarded as especially appropriate.

At around the time that Samwell's thoughts had turned towards the South Seas he took a small but significant step in asserting his own identity. He changed the spelling of his surname from Samuel to Samwell. He explained this briefly and with his usual measure of flippancy to Gregson: 'My name is always pronounced Samwell in Wales. if my Grandfather did not know how to spell his name properly that is no reason why I shou'd put up with such a damn'd Israelitish one as Samuel.'[28] Samwell may have got tired of being asked whether he was a Jew, a question which might have been encouraged not only by his name but also by his black hair. Later he would choose for his bardic name Dafydd ddu Feddyg, 'Black David the Doctor'.[29] The revised spelling of his surname was English, for in Welsh it would require only one 'l'; pronounced as a Welsh name, Samwell would sound something like 'Samweth'.[30] So it was his own independent identity he was asserting, rather than a cultural identity. Appropriately, Samwell the independent adventurer in life would soon receive his great break, and that he owed to John Crosier.

John Crosier thought highly of Samwell, but he was no doubt aware of his hot temper and bouts of extravagant behaviour. With such tendencies, he could easily have fallen into a low-life existence, quite possibly as a hack writer, as he had already published in the *Sentimental Magazine* and the *Westminster Magazine*.[31] However, Crosier had high hopes for him. Within months of his qualifying as a surgeon, he had secured Samwell a position as surgeon's mate on the *Resolution* in a new expedition to the South Seas. First he solicited his former shipmate, Charles Clerke, and then, when Cook was formally appointed captain of the expedition on 10 February, he petitioned him, so that Samwell's status was upgraded to surgeon's first mate. The second mate appointed to replace him was Samwell's schoolmate, Robert Davies from Mold, who had only just qualified as surgeon's mate.[32] Samwell was aware that Crosier's confidence in him was dependent on his good behaviour. He wrote to Gregson on 25 March 1776, 'Mr Crosier has been the best of friends to me & has promised always to be such while I behave well'. On his return, Samwell hoped he would become a surgeon. Crosier had faith in his apprentice, despite his wayward tendencies. When he heard the news despatched by Cook from Kamchatka that William Anderson, the surgeon on the *Resolution*, had died, he correctly predicted that Samwell would have been promoted.[33] Following the death of Anderson, on 5 August, 1778, John Law, surgeon to the *Discovery*, took over his position, and Samwell was appointed as surgeon to the *Discovery* in Law's place. He seems to enjoyed a reputation as a competent surgeon, and was extremely proud of the fact that not a single sailor was lost on the *Discovery* through sickness – in marked contrast with the high wastage rates in the British navy at the time.[34]

Samwell returned from Cook's last expedition a more interesting man, if not a wealthier one. Writing in his *Journal* of the Indian women of Nootka Sound, which the expedition visited in April 1778, he explained that many on the expedition had already exchanged all their available hatchets and nails for the 'beautiful nymphs' in the South Seas and so were driven to exchange their 'kitchen furniture' for the 'fair Americans'. He explained, 'we enjoyed the present Day & left the Morrow to provide for itself – & to provide us Tables & Chests to eat our Salt Beef & pork from instead of Plates'.[35] Not all Samwell's trade was for sexual favours, and he brought back a sufficient number of artefacts to hold an auction of them in 1781.[36] The proceeds perhaps enabled him to devote some time to improving his skills as a surgeon. In the winter of 1781 he attended the anatomy classes of Drs Hunter and Fordyce. His situation also became more assured when he received the good news that the Admiralty had placed him on the list of naval surgeons from the date of Cook's warrant (4 August 1778). Samwell attributed this more to Cook's posthumous influence than to his own merit. It was important to him, as it affected the length of service which would be credited to him and brought nearer the day when he could retire on half-pay, which would be after seven years' service. [37]

Soon after hearing this news he returned to the sea, for the simple reason that if he stayed on land he thought he might starve. Yet the sea was not without its attractions. He enlisted under Captain King on the *Crocodile*, 'a beautiful little frigate'. He liked and respected King, and many of those who had also served on Cook's last expedition joined his ship, so many that it was rumoured that they were off on another voyage of discovery. In fact, they were engaged in hostilities with French ships fighting as allies of the rebel American colonies. Samwell rather enjoyed combat at sea, and always had an eye to his share in prize-money. But his main objective was to retire on half-pay, and so he continued to serve in the navy following the peace in 1783. He had completed sufficient service by the end of 1786 and he retired to live in Fetter Lane, in the heart of London.[38] He hoped to live the life of 'a gentleman at large'. He developed what one presumes was a modest private medical practice. In this period he became a member of the Medical Society of London and could put M. M. L. after his name.[39] He explained to Gregson that it was common for a private practice to start with high expectations and to achieve early results. These were not easy to sustain; fifteen years into a practice one might find one-self back where one started. The unwillingness of Samwell to tell his friend in a letter whether he was making 'money fast' suggests that he was having some initial success. [40] Nonetheless, his navy pension relieved him of the pressure to make a steady income from medicine. He may not have achieved the lifestyle of a gentleman, but he had sufficient leisure time to become closely involved in Welsh cultural activity. He became secretary of the Gwyneddigion Society in 1787, and vice-president ten years later. He assisted his friends in collecting the works of Dafydd ap Gwilym, and he himself wrote a *Sketch of the Life and Writings of Hugh Morris* (1795). [41] In 1792 he was one of the four presiding bards at a Gorsedd of Bards held at Primrose Hill, London. Shortly before his death he was actively promoting an eisteddfod at Caerwys.

In the closing years of his life, Samwell, well known in Welsh circles, had also achieved a minor degree of fame as a poet in English. Samwell's letters to Gregson show that he sought the company of poets when he first went to Liverpool. He was reading the work of the future Mrs Barbauld when her father was teaching at the nearby Warrington Academy, and he came to know personally the Rational Dissenter William Roscoe. He objected when Roscoe compared painters to the sons of Apollo, for he argued, 'There is no Art or Profession under the Sun, that ought to be hinted at, as a comparison with heaven inspired poetry.'[42] As well as publishing occasional pieces throughout his career, Samwell wrote poetry for his personal pleasure, and he included some of his efforts in his letters to Gregson. After his return from the Pacific, he came to know Anna Seward, who had composed a popular 'Elegy on Captain Cook' (1780). Her letters to him indicate a high degree of mutual respect and a vigorous critical discussion of contemporary poets. She placed him in the camp of humanitarian poets, a view confirmed by his 'The Negro Boy' as well as the 'Ode for New Year' of 1790, and held him in high esteeem: 'Rays of genius play over the paper', she wrote of one of Samwell's letters, and reminded him that critics thought him worthy of the Poet Laureateship. [43]

Samwell's association with Cook had brought him Seward's friendship, but although he did gain some recognition from his association he did not seek to exploit it. Through the encouragement of his Liverpool friends, he had kept a journal of his voyage with Cook. He may have written this with the intention of publication, but when he returned he was extremely cautious about showing it to friends. This can be explained by the Admiralty prohibition on publications concerning the voyage until the official account was published, by Samwell's desire not to harm his prospects in the navy, and by his feeling that it might in some ways be construed as harmful to the memory of Cook, whom he adored. [44] Whatever he meant by that, he was at least persuaded to write an account of Cook's death and an assessment of his life and character for Andrew Kippis. Kippis was an enormously influential figure in the late eighteenth-century English Enlightenment, not only for his teaching and his publications but because of his network of influence amongst printers and publishers which he had built up over many years. One of Samwell's Liverpool friends and fellow bards was George Gregory. Much to Samwell's surprise, while he was voyaging with Cook, Gregory went to Edinburgh University to study divinity. He was then ordained in the Anglican Church and took up a ministry in London. With his literary and theatrical interests he came to know Kippis. The latter was in the process of preparing a new edition of the *Biographia Britannica* and was approaching the letter C. He required information on crucial matters relating to Cook and his voyages, and it is likely that Gregory acted as an intermediary between Kippis and Samwell. Kippis liked Samwell's account so much that he proposed its separate publication. The pamphlet, published here, appeared in 1786 and was translated into French in the same year. However, Kippis himself gave Samwell's views much greater currency by incorporating them into his own *A Narrative of the*

Voyages Round the World Performed by Captain James Cook with an Account of his Life . . . (1788). This was a substantial work which, whatever its limitations, provided the standard account of the life of Cook until the twentieth century. We have traced forty-eight editions of the work from 1788 until 1925. There were nineteen editions published in Britain and Europe before the end of the eighteenth century. Samwell himself described the work as 'The best written abridgement of Captn Cook's voyages of any that have been published'. [45] Crosier thought that the best part was that written by Samwell. Samwell disagreed. He had, however, played a substantial part in the creation of the enlightened image of Cook. Not only did Kippis include his account of the death of Cook, but in his conclusion, or perhaps one should say peroration, for Kippis was a Dissenting minister, he gave prominence to Samwell's assessment of Cook's character, quoting it almost verbatim. The impact of Kippis's work awaits close study, but Samwell at least discovered that he had gained some modest recognition. Immediately, one of Crosier's friends, a surgeon at St Thomas's hospital, asked to be introduced to him. He was as impressed as Crosier with Samwell's contribution, and invited him to attend his hospital. Several years later, in 1795, Samwell heard of the discovery of new Shakespearean manuscripts. It was public knowledge that the owner of the manuscript, a Mr Ireland, was willing to show it to interested gentlemen. Samwell, a great Shakespearean enthusiast, without arranging an introduction went forthwith to inspect the manuscript. He received a rather frosty reception, until, spotting the *Biographia Britannica* on a shelf, he was able to point out his contribution to the fourth volume and that he had travelled with Cook. He was immediately treated as a fêted guest. [46]

Such episodes may have given Samwell some comfort for a life not quite fulfilled. Although the 1790s were exciting times and Samwell was kept busy, he had bouts of drinking and drug-taking which may have been indicative of self-disappointment, and which may have taken a toll on his health. The evidence is not conclusive, since he was not alone in such activities. His great friend, Iolo Morganwg, regularly took opium, in the form of laudanum, and wrote an ode on its effects. [47] He died in his eighty-first year. One of Samwell's friends, Owain Myfyr, did think that over-indulgence in drink and laudanum contributed towards his death. [48] Samwell, was, however, at sea for a good part of the 1790s. He would have had plenty of beer and grog on board, but drunkenness was a punishable offence. His letters to Gregson do not provide any real evidence of decline, or of the self-pity that often goes with it. What we do know is that Samwell died suddenly, according to Anna Seward, of 'apolexy', probably a stroke or possibly a heart attack. [49] He died at a time when he reported that he was in good health, and the engraving of 1798 would appear to bear that out.[50] We also know that at this time, as a man in his forties, he reflected on the way his life had gone and whether he could have done better for himself. From quite early on he had a sense that he would not be very good at handling his career; his later reflections confirmed his intuition. In confiding his thoughts to his long-time friend in 1795, he was anxious that he should understand that for him there was no higher ambition or station than that of surgeon, which was the 'summit of his profession'. [51] His regrets were about the way he had promoted his career as a surgeon. He was not good at self-promotion, and his best opportunities came as a result of Crosier's influence. In particular, Samwell blamed himself for not taking an opportunity which Croiser put his way in 1783. It is worth quoting a key passage from one of his letters, because they betray his feelings at this time; they are wistful, but not self-indulgent:

> I enjoy very good health at sea but do not care how soon peace comes, for I am almost tire'd of such a foolish and unprofitable kind of life – in following which, I cannot help considering myself as in a manner thrown away – or in plain terms, feeling myself much superior to the station I am in – this give me disagreeable sensations at times, but they are transitory, for, the Lord be praised, Nature never designed I should grieve at any thing. Leaving the Marlborough was of (?) no consequence in the world tho' I could have wished much to have been in the action, and I have been told since that the officers wished so too – there is only one *Miss* I made in the Navy. which was this – from Crosier's application the present Lord Bridport during the American War offer'd to get me appointed to his ship the Queen of 90 guns. Not one in the service but myself would have been so silly as to decline it – for no other reason in the world but that I was agreeably situated with my messmates in the Pegase – the surgeon who was lucky enough to get what I refused, was appointed through his Lordship's interest surgeon of Plymouth dockyard, about six months ago – worth about 500£ a year. I could not forsee this to be sure – and as it cannot be help'd I don't mind it – only give it you as an anecdote of my folly or whatever you please to call it – . . . [52]

Samwell had returned to the sea with the outbreak of war with France in January 1793, but was naturally envious of the well-paid post on dry land which might have been his.[53] The awful wintry conditions of 1794 so well captured in his Christmas Day 'Ode' of 1794 must have heightened the regrets which he expressed the following year. Gregson was anxious to do what he could to help his friend; Samwell in turn tried to allay his anxiety, telling him that he would be content enough to win a little more prize-money and retire to his home and practice in Fetter Lane. [54] Then, out of the blue, in 1798, he was presented with a golden opportunity to end his career on a more satisfactory note. A notice appeared in the papers indicating that under a new arrangement four agents and four navy surgeons were to be appointed to serve the needs of British prisoners-of-war in France. Samwell was attracted both by the opportunity to serve on dry land and by the pay, which, at a guinea a day, was better than any appointment on board ship. However, he did not think he had much of a chance and did not canvass for the position, writing instead his application in a perfunctory three lines. To his surprise and delight he was appointed. Samwell loved cities and so he chose to serve at Versailles, so that he could get to know Paris. He had his own servant, or 'man Friday', as he called him, and by the time he wrote, at the end of May 1798, he had hired a first-floor apartment. He was in fine spirits, reporting that he 'never was in better health'. He was able to move around freely, provided he wore the French national cockade in his hat; lest his friend thought 'that for once I am a prudent man in so doing, no such thing – every body in France is obliged to put it in his hat, or be stopped by the sentries &c'.[55]

So far as we know that was Samwell's last letter to his lifetime friend. It was not the letter of a disillusioned man, but of Samwell the adventurer who was enjoying a new set of experiences, and who was, as ever, able to laugh at himself. He returned to London in September, and died at home, in Fetter Lane, on 23 November.

Notes

[1] Samuel Johnson, *A Dictionary of the English Language . . . Abstracted From the Folio Edition by the Author Samuel Johnson, A. M.*, in two volumes, the seventh edition corrected by the author (London 1783), vol. 1.

[2] Davies, 'David Samwell', 73; the school statutes at Ruthin, 'encouraged pupils to rehearse Latin drama', see William P. Griffith, 'Humanist Learning, Education and the Welsh language 1536–1660', in Geraint Jenkins (ed.), *The Welsh Language before the Industrial Revolution* (Cardiff: University of Wales Press, 1997), pp. 289–316 (p. 300).

[3] Griffith, 'Humanist learning', p.307.

[4] Davies, 'David Samwell', app. I, 128–9.

[5] See Robert E. Gallagher (ed.), *Byron's Journal of Circumnavigation, 1764–66* (Cambridge: Hakluyt Society, 1964), pp. lxxi–lxxii, 3–9. Byron's brief was to search for undiscovered lands in the South Atlantic 'within latitudes convenient for Navigation' and to search for the North-West Passage.

[6] His familiarity with the Wirral is confirmed in a letter from Anna Seward, 17 March 1795; A. Constable (ed.), *Letters of Anna Seward Written Between the Years 1784 and 1807* (Edinburgh: [unidentified publisher], 1811), IV, p. 37.

[7] Letter 7, to Matthew Gregson, 15 December 1774, Liverpool Record Office 920 GRE 2117. The correspondence is hereafter referred to by Letter (followed by a number), Samwell to Gregson unless noted otherwise. In this letter, cited in the text (n.15), if one follows Samwell's dating exactly, he was referring to the

by-election in December 1767 by which Pennant was returned. No poll was held, as his opponent John Tarleton withdrew his opposition in October. Samwell could be referring to those preliminaries when the rival candidates sized each other up. Alternatively, he might have been referring to the preliminaries a few months later at the general election. Pennant was again returned unopposed, but there were rumbustious manoeuvrings prior to the March election. Tarleton was forced to abandon the contest by the violence of the Greenland fishermen. F. O'Gorman, *Voter, Patrons and Parties: The Unreformed Electoral System of Hanoverian England 1734–1832* (Oxford: Oxford University Press, 1989), p. 257 citing a report in the *Liverpool Chronicle*, 24 March, 1768; Sir Lewis Namier and John Brooke, *The House of Commons 1754–1790* (London: H. M. S. O. , 1964), I, p. 3178.

8　Richard Pennant, Baron Penrhyn (1737?–1808), MP for Liverpool 1767 to 1790. He was descended from Thomas ap Dafydd, abbot of Basingwerk in the fifteenth century, as was Thomas Pennant. Later in his career, he would develop slate quarrying at Penrhyn, in North Wales (information from *DNB*).

9　Letter 7, 15 December 1774.

10　Samwell made two inscriptions in his edition of Horace, one inscribed 'Greenland May 24 1771', the other, 'America July 20th 1778', when he was in the Bering Sea with Cook looking for a north-west passage. Davies, 'David Samwell', p. 73; Beaglehole, *Journals*, p. 1128.

11　Letter 1, June 12 1772. It is clear from this letter that this is not the first letter in their correspondence.

12　J. Hunter, 'Notices of Contemporaries, 1827–36', British Library, Add. MS 36527, f.167, dated 25 September 1834. They dined in May 1821.

13　There is a reference to a 'Mrs Meddyg Du' in a letter of 23 December 1791 from Iolo Morganwg to William Owen, NLW [National Library of Wales] 13224B no.1, pp. 1–2. There is no other evidence to suggest that Samwell was married. Iolo's reference was probably jocular; it is quite likely that at the time Samwell did have a close female companion.

14　Letter 13, 16 May 1776; Letter 15, 12 July 1776; Letter 25, 26 February 1781.

15　Letter 47, 30 June 1794; Letter 48, 16 July 1794. Samwell supplied several variations, and the Christian name was an insertion rather than essential.

16　Hunter, 'Notices of Contemporaries', f.167: 'I am told he was an auctioneer or upholsterer. I am told in about 1785 he was pursuing his medical studies in London.' There is no evidence for this in the correspondence, where the only clue is some light-hearted banter from Samwell in a letter of 1 May 1775 (Letter 8).

17　The second and third letters were addressed to Gregson at Mr Urmson's Upholstry Shop, then the fourth letter, of 25 March 1774, was addressed to Gregson at Mrs Urmson's Upholstry Shop. Presumably her husband had died and she had taken over the business. Perhaps she sold it to Gregson. His shop, at any rate, was in the same street, Castle Street, but from letter 10, 9 December 1775, Mrs Urmson no longer appears on his address.

18　Gallagher (ed.), *Byron's Journal of Circumnavigation*, pp. 88, 143–4.

19　Hawkesworth, *An Account of the Voyages*.

20   Byron's vessel the *Dolphin* was immediately used again by Wallis, while his
      unfortunate companion, Carteret, commanded an old sloop in poor condition.
      After they entered the Pacific, the two ships parted, but Carteret, remarkably,
      completed his voyage, returning almost a year after Wallis. The *Dolphin* under
      Wallis made the European discovery of Tahiti, in June 1767. The early phase of
      contact was controversially violent, but peace was eventually made, and a
      good relationship formed with the prominent woman Purea, called 'Oberea'
      by the British and erroneously believed to be queen of the island. The positive
      reports of Wallis and other crew members prompted the choice of Tahiti as the
      site for Cook's observation of the 1769 Transit of Venus. and hence were
      decisive in shaping the subsequent pattern of European contact in Polynesia.
21   Letter 3, 24 June 1773.
22   Letter 5, 25 June 1774.
23   W. H. Pearson, 'Hawkesworth's *Voyages*', in R. F. Brissenden (ed.) *Studies in the
      Eighteenth Century* (Canberra: Australian National University Press, 1973),
      pp. 239–57, at (p. 240).
24   Hawkesworth, *An Account of the Voyage*, I, pp. 28–32; see also Gallagher (ed.),
      Byron's Journal of Circumnavigation, pp. lxxvii-lxxx, 46 and illustration opposite
      the page, taken from *A Voyage round the World in His Majesty's Ship the Dolphin
      . . . by an officer on board the said ship* (1767); and in the same volume, Helen
      Wallis's essay, 'The Patagonian Giants', pp. 185–96; Helen Wallis, *Carteret's Voyage
      Round the World, 1766–1769* (Cambridge: Hakluyt Society, 1965), pp. 461–76;
      Pearson, 'Hawkesworth's *Voyages*'.
25   One of those who contributed to the debate was Charles Clerke, with whom
      Crosier remained on friendly terms. Clerke wrote an account which he sub-
      mitted to the Royal Society and which was subsequently published in their
      Philosophical Transactions. His account was highly exaggerated, so much so
      that Beaglehole thinks that Clarke's intent may well have been satirical. If so,
      Samwell would have enjoyed the joke. Wallis, 'The Patagonian Giants', p. 188,
      n.4.
26   The society soon admitted Welshmen from south Wales. William Davies Leathart,
      The Origins and Progress of the Gwyneddigion Society of London (London, Hugh
      Pierce Hughes, 1831), p. 12; Prys Morgan, *The Eighteenth Century Renaissance*
      (Llandybïe: Christopher Davies, 1981), pp. 61–2.
27   Hawkesworth, *Voyages*, plates 3, 4, 7. For extensive discussion of the classic-
      ization of Pacific subjects see Bernard Smith, *European Vision and the South
      Pacific*, second edn. (New Haven: Yale University Press, 1985).
28   Letter 8, 1 May 1775; the first letter which he signed Samwell was Letter 6,
      14 September 1774.
29   Members of the Gwyneddigion Society assumed cognomens partly to distin-
      guish members with the same surnames, but they were also descriptive of
      personal features. Because of his black hair, Samwell was know as 'Myddyg
      du', the dark or black doctor. His bardic identity naturally followed from that.
      It also helped to distinguish him from another Dafydd Ddu who was from
      Snowdonia, namely Dafydd ddu Eryri. Leathart, *The Origins and Progress*,
      pp. 15–16.

30 Leathart in *The Origins and Progress* spelt his name in the Welsh way as Samwel, as did some of his Welsh contemporaries. It is not the spelling which Samwell himself adopted.

31 Letter 4, 25 March 1774; Letter 5, 25 June 1774.

32 Samwell felt that the position was fairly well secured when he wrote to Gregson on 25 December 1775. However, it was not until 15 February 1776 that he received his warrant as surgeon's second mate; that was upgraded to surgeon's first mate on 22 March (Letter 10, 25 December 1775; Letter 11, 23 February 1776; Letter 12, 25 March 1776). Davies and Samwell were two of the five known Welshmen on the expedition. Beaglehole, *Journals*, pp. 1457, 1463, 1465.

33 See Letter 13, 16 May 1776; Letter 17, 2 February 1780.

34 Letter 22, 16 December 1780; Letter 23, to Mr Christie, 17 December 1780. On the voyage home, Samwell successfully treated ship's carpenter's mate William Walker for a broken arm. Henry Zimmermann, *Voyage Round the World with Captain Cook* (1781), trans U. Tewsley (Wellington: Alexander Turnbull Library, 1926), p. 43; Beaglehole, *Journals*, p. 1472.

35 Beaglehole, *Journals*, pp. 1094–6.

36 Adrienne L. Kaeppler, 'Tracing the History of Hawaiian Cook Voyage Artefacts in the Museum of Mankind', in T. C. Mitchell (ed.), *Captain Cook and the South Pacific* (London: British Museum Press, 1979), pp. 167–97, (pp. 173, 175, pls. 96, 97). A Hawaiian drum (see p.61 this volume) and a New Zealand Maori flax beater made of stone, at the Hunterian Museum and Art Gallery, University of Glasgow, are thought to have been acquired by William Hunter from David Samwell. Hunter may have bought them at Samwell's 1781 auction or received them from Samwell directly; Samwell was intending to spend time with Hunter in the winter of 1780–1 (see p. 106 this volume). Leathart (*Origins and Progress*, pp. 30–1n.) wrote that part of Samwell's collection was eventually deposited in the library of Trinity College Cambridge. However, the only materials deposited in the library came from Cook's first voyage, given by Cook to the Earl of Sandwich and by Sandwich to Trinity in October 1771. They are now housed in the Museum of Archaeology and Anthropology. I am grateful for this information to the Trinity College Archivist, Jonathan Smith.

37 Letter 26, 7 April 1781.

38 Samwell's first address in Fetter Lane was no. 22 but within the year he had moved to no. 117, 'a much better house', formerly a grocer's shop. Letter 39, 7 July 1787; Letter 41, 11 October 1788.

39 The Medical Society of London had been founded recently, in 1773. Abraham Hume, *The Learned Societies and Printing Clubs of the United Kingdom . . .* (London: G. Willis, 1853), pp. 100–1.

40 Letter 42, 15 October 1788.

41 Davies, 'David Samwell', pp. 97–8.

42 Letter 5, 25 June 1774.

43 Letters of Anna Seward, III, pp. 139–40, Seward to Samwell, 12 December 1795. Seward was interested in the Welsh cultural revival. Samwell may have been responsible for her investiture as an ovate of the Order of Welsh Bards in the autumn of 1793 (Davies, 'David Samwell (1751–1798)', 119 n.1).

44   Letter 25, 26 February 1781. The Admiralty instructed the Navy Board on
     16 October 1780 to send the journals and logbooks of the voyages to them for
     inspection. National Maritime Museum, Greenwich, ADM/A/2756.
45   Letter 41, 11 October 1788; Letter 42, 15 October 1788.
46   Letter 49, 9 August 1795. The 'Mr Ireland' was not a lawyer, as Samwell thought,
     but Samuel Ireland (d.1800), a weaver and a successful self-taught engraver.
     Samwell immediately pronounced the manuscripts to be authentic, although
     he had seen only a facsimile of Shakepeare's hand. They were in fact forgeries,
     made by Ireland's son, William Henry Ireland (1777–1825). The father had
     been anxious to have them authenticated, and in February 1795 invited men
     of literary distinction to examine them. The manuscripts were available for
     inspection for a year, and during that period leading literary figures had
     pronounced in Ireland's favour. Doubts grew in 1796, and eventually the son
     confessed to having forged them. Sadly, the father refused to credit his nineteen-
     year-old son with such skills and became the target of the anger of a gullible
     public. Anna Seward had queried Samwell's conviction of authenticity; see
     Letters of Anna Seward, IV, pp. 37–8, Seward to Samwell, 17 March 1795.
47   On occasion Samwelll supplied Iolo with laudanum. National Library of Wales
     MSS 21282E, Letters 458, 458a.
48   Davies, 'David Samwell', p. 122.
49   Letters of Anna Seward, V, p. 196, Seward to Miss Ponsonby, 24 January 1799.
50   Gwyn A. Williams provides no evidence for his suggestion that Samwell died
     of venereal disease (and in France) (*Madoc: The Making of a Legend*, London:
     Eyre and Methuen, 1979, p. 5).
51   Letter 51, 8 October 1795.
52   Letter 49, 9 August 1795. See also Letter 34, 6 January 1783. Lord Bridport was
     Alexander Hood (1758–98). In September 1782 he was appointed to command
     the grand fleet under Lord Howe. His flagship was the *Queen*, in which
     Samwell had the opportunity of serving. He was elevated to the Irish peerage
     on 12 August 1794.
53   Samwell had told Gregson when he set up his practice that he would be
     obliged to leave it were war to break out. Letter 41, 11 October 1788.
54   Letter 50, 1 October 1795; Letter 51, 8 October 1795.
55   Letter 54, 31 May 1798.

2

David Samwell on his hobby horse

MARTIN FITZPATRICK

David Samwell's obituary in the *Gentleman's Magazine* indicates the minor eminence he had achieved and the associations which he left in the public mind. It is also indicative of his literary achievements in both English and Welsh:

> Dec. 1798. At his house in Fetter – lane, aged 47. Mr David Samwell, surgeon in His Majesty's navy. He accompanied Capt. Cook in his last voyage to the South Seas; and, a few years ago, published an account of the circumstances attending the death of that celebrated navigator. He was likewise author of many short detached pieces of poetry, as well in his native Welsh as in the English language; several of which have appeared in our miscellany, and possess considerable merit. His little poem of 'The Negro boy' was favourably received by the publick. He was a man of cultivated understanding and friendly disposition. In his profession he was justly esteemed skilful; and he is much lamented. [1]

Those who knew Samwell would have recognized only half the man in this obituary. For someone so full of life, so full of contradictions, it is somewhat bland. To his friends, he could be infuriating and puzzling. He was in many ways quite brilliant, wonderfully entertaining company, but someone who could explode. It is true that only his close friends and drinking companions really experienced his dazzling intelligence and his waywardness, but even those who knew him less well could see that he was a talented and many-sided person. His death even at the relatively mature age of forty-seven seemed premature, for in today's parlance he seemed to have underachieved. Few of his contemporaries knew of his superb journal of Cook's third voyage, nor were they to know that in Kippis's *Life and Voyages of Cook*, Samwell's account of Cook's death and his assessment of his character would live on for over a century and would be published forty-eight times in all. One at least of his Welsh contemporaries summed up the feelings of some of Samwell's friends on his death when he remarked appositely that 'where there's genius, there'll be chaos'.[2] His contemporaries certainly found difficulty in understanding and assessing this man of so many apparent contradictions. Although these cannot be smoothed out, we can take a journey round the man and explore his complexities in an attempt to understand his travels through life.

Samwell delighted in every new experience and every new challenge. He did not embark with Cook as a result of a long-held ambition to journey to the South Seas; he was an opportunist and adventurer, loving every new challenge which presented itself. He relished the moment, and loved to convey his experiences in his letters. Typical of his exuberant personality was the occasion when the Italian balloonist, Vincenzo Lunardi, flew along the Thames through London Bridge. Samwell joined a group who had hired a boat to follow the balloon. When they approached the bridge, he asked the boatman why he had stopped following the balloon. He was met with the reply, 'What have you a mind to run the risk of losing your life?' Samwell's rejoinder was, 'To be sure on such a glorious expedition as this'. Second only to the excitement of such expeditions was writing about them. In typical tongue-in-cheek way, he wrote that such incidents helped 'a fellow of no invention and fancy to eke out a long letter'. [3] He then spelt out his epistolary philosophy: 'Nothing vexes me more than a letter filled with common news that are always more amply discussed in the Papers'. Voyaging with Cook was a gift to such writer. Even in the periods when he pursued a medical career on dry land, Samwell was always seeking out new experiences and pouring his energy into his latest enthusiasms. Most of these were not, like the Lunardi episode, whims and opportunities of the moment, but arose from his interests and wider concerns. These to a degree gave shape to his irregular life and unusual career.

Any attempt to understand Samwell must start with his Celtic roots. He was proud of his Welshness, and he made a distinctive contribution to the Welsh linguistic and literary renaissance of the late eighteenth century. As the son of a cleric, he would have been aware of the damaging effects of Anglicization. The eighteenth-century Welsh Church suffered from an impoverished Welsh clergy and an episcopate which was incapable of speaking to its flock in their own language. Although the needs of Welsh-speaking congregations were generally met, Welsh clerics had a poor deal. English was the language of preferment, and there was a growing social prejudice against the language amongst many of the Welsh squirearchy, who regarded Welsh as a vulgar tongue.

There is no mention of the harmful impact of Anglicization on Welsh culture and religion in Samwell's letters to the Englishman Gregson. Perhaps one should not expect it; he was not someone who harboured resentment, nor was he a conventional Anglican. [4] He would make amusing references to his country's traditions and the quirks of the behaviour of the Welsh. When writing from Portsmouth in 1781, he noted that 'Cockcades

are as thick here as leeks in a Welshman's garden'.[5] Then, not long before
his death, he wrote, 'I begin to jabber a little French & hope soon to be
able to forget my Welsh & English according to the laudable custom of
some of our ingenious countrymen who visit England, forget *yr hên famiath*
& sometimes forget to learn any other instead of it . . .'.[6] Samwell, of
course, had no intention of losing his old mother tongue (*yr hên famiath*),
and worked hard to ensure the vitality of Welsh culture. Yet considering
his deep commitment, his preference for irony over condemnation of his
backsliding fellow countrymen says a good deal about the man.

In some ways Samwell can be regarded as a Welsh nationalist, but one
has to be careful to understand what that means. The term nationalist was
not one which was recognized in his lifetime, and only late in the century
did nation, with its democratic connotations, come to rival country as the
focus of patriotism. It was the exaltation of '*La Nation*' by the French
revolutionaries which gave real impetus to this trend. The process can be
seen in the Welsh language. The lexicographer, John Walters, coined the
Welsh word for patriotism, *gwladgarwch*, in 1776. The word is a composite
of 'love of country'. An alternative came into use in the 1790s, *cenedligrwydd*,
meaning nationality. Samwell at one time regarded himself in self-conscious
terms as a patriot. He soon rejected this, but not because of unease about
being Welsh rather than British; rather, he came to reject aspects of patriotism associated with the reform movement which John Wilkes championed.
It was this patriotism which Dr. Johnson described as the 'last refuge of a
scoundrel'. Yet Samwell remained a patriot in a less specific sense, and
was proud to be both Welsh and British. For him, the very Welshness of
the Welsh proved that they were the most British of the British for they
were the descendants of the ancient Britons or, as they sometimes described
themselves, the Aboriginal Britons.[7] In 1789, his fellow countryman, Richard
Price, preached the most important discussion of patriotism at that time,
his *Discourse on the Love of our Country*. It created a furore and led Edmund
Burke to reply with his *Reflections on the Revolution in France* (1790).
Samwell shared Price's enthusiasm for the French Revolution and for
reform at home, and also the uplifting conviction of the time, captured in
his own 'New Year Ode' of 1790, that 'the ardor for liberty' was 'catching
and spreading'.[8] Yet his patriotism had cultural and instinctive elements,
missing in Price's essentially rational analysis. They were, however, quite
complex. One might expect that man who thought of home on St David's
Day, 1 March 1777, while sailing from New Zealand to Tahiti, would have
special feelings for the landscape of home, feelings of the sort which would
become characteristic of romantic nationalism. As one can see from his
description of the Hawaiian landscape as 'forming a Prospect highly picturesque and romantic',[9] he was conversant with the aesthetic norms of the

picturesque traveller, but appreciation of hills and waterfalls did not mean
he had a sentimental attachment to those of Wales. He was devoted to Wales
as a place because of its history and myths. Moreover, a key feature of his
patriotism was his attachment to those with whom he associated. Burke
described the primary constituent of patriotism as love of 'the little platoon
we belong to in society'. The metaphor is a military one, for a platoon is
the small defensive square of musketeers formed from foot-soldiers of a
battalion. [10] Naturally, it can be interpreted in different ways, but it fits
Samwell in the sense that he was a profoundly loyal person, and there was
a fierce pride and aggressive edge to the various forms of his patriotism,
as there was to the man. It was not defence of land which mattered to him,
but defence of those with whom he conversed, and of the things which
they thought worth discussing. In thinking of home on St David's Day, he
thought of his Welsh friends in the Gwyneddigion Society in London. [11]
Samwell was a London Welshman by choice. He was consistent in this,
preferring London to the allure of Paris, or the infinitely different charms
of the South Seas. When he inherited land in north Wales, he contemplated
selling it. Although that proved to be impossible, his attitude was quite
hard-headed: 'Money in the funds would be more productive than those
acres.' This was in 1794, when he was having trouble with the lease of his
house in London. He did not entirely rule out moving back to Wales, but
his lack of enthusiasm made it highly unlikely. He wrote to Gregson: 'So if
I should neither go to sea nor remain in London, I may take a view of the
Welsh Mounts. but I daresay shall soon get tired of them, "tower'd Cities
please us then, An the busy hum of Men".'[12] A year later when Gregson
was hoping to purchase a house in the Vale of Clwyd, Samwell replied,
'give me a house in Fetter Lane, say I, Matthew – How various our taste'.[13]

The little Welsh platoon that Samwell loved was made up of like-minded
Welshmen, especially those from north Wales. These were lovers of the
Welsh language and literature. Samwell called his friends who were poets,
'bards', whether they composed in Welsh or English. The word had associations with ancient traditions of versifying and mythologizing which
appealed to eighteenth-century sentimentalists, not least to Samwell. The
cult of the bards had been stimulated by Thomas Gray's poem *The Bard*
(1757). Gray envisages the last surviving bard defying the elements on a
mountain outcrop, with his 'beard and hoary hair' streaming 'like a meteor
to the troubled air'. On his lyre, he strikes up a lament to the army of
Llywelyn the Great, which had been defeated by the forces of the English
king, Edward I. As it ends, he plunges headlong into an abyss. The theme
of the oppressor is thus intimately bound up with bardic ideas. Edward
was 'Cambria's curse', and Cambria's revival was a revival of the spirit of
the oppressed. There are obvious parallels between this sort of primitivism

and that of radicals who believed that through the proper study of the ancient past, and the effective propagation of its results Englishmen would be able to recover their lost rights. This was the purpose of the Society for Constitutional Information, set up in 1780, which assumed that the abstract rights of men were one and the same with the historic rights which Englishmen supposedly enjoyed under the Anglo-Saxon Constitution. Equally, there are theological analogues in the belief that one could strip away the corruptions of Christianity and reveal it in its true nature. This was the avowed intent of Joseph Priestley, whose theology became steadily more Unitarian. Samwell, with his early sympathy with John Wilkes and interest in Unitarianism, was attracted by this conjunction of ideas. Soon after Theophilus Lindsey opened the first avowedly Unitarian Chapel in Essex Street, off the Strand, London, Samwell attended a service. Lindsey used a reformed Anglican liturgy. All these elements in Samwell's make-up can be seen within the space of a few lines in a letter written to Gregson at the time of the general election of 1774:

> You have heard of the honour paid Lady Lewes at Worcester – Sr. Watkyn most certainly acquitted himself like an ancient Briton in the Affair of that Election & if he is not chosen their Representative in the ensuing Parliament, we may very fairly say that there are but few independent Electors in England. [14]
>
> I have heard the proto martyr the revd. Mr Theophilus Lindsey & approve him. I think that the alteration he had made in the Common Prayer are done with Judgement. I may in another letter take notice of one which reflects Honour upon him both as a Freeman & and Englishman. There will be a hard contest this year for the Mayoralty. I am in great hopes Wilkes will get it. [15]

Samwell was by no means alone in approving of ancient British virtue and purified religion. His friend Edward Williams, Iolo Morganwg, shared these values, and did more than any other Welshman to revive and re-create them. Yet before he made his own signal contribution, the Gwyneddigion Society had already been formed for the promotion of Welsh culture, and it encouraged the holding of eisteddfods for this purpose. These had a libertarian ethos – the subject for the *awdl* and the prose essay at the Llanelwy (St Asaph) Eisteddfod on 25 May 1790 was 'Liberty'. Gwallter Mechain (Walter Davies) carried off the prize for the prose essay, and his essay was subsequently published. These were the heady early years of the French Revolution, when Samwell joined the celebrations for the fall of the Bastille and moved in radical circles, including that of Helen Maria Williams, whom he would later stay with in Paris, and when Thomas Paine published his *Rights of Man* (1791–92), a work which Samwell would revere alongside the works of Shakespeare.[16] For a time, British radicalism and Welsh cultural revivalism seemed all of a piece.

One of the most interesting and transitory features of the Welsh revival was the attempt to interest the English in it by making English an official language. In 1792, the first Gorsedd of Bards to be held in London, on Primrose Hill, designated English a bardic language as well as Welsh. [17] In keeping with the modish antiquarian radicalism, it set as the topic for the English Ode to be composed for the next meeting, '*The Resurrection of* RHITTA GAWR', explaining that 'RHITTA GAWR was a famous chief of the *Ancient Britons*, who exterminated so many despots that he made himself a robe of their beards'. [18]

Another aspect of this type of radicalism was its adherence to pacific doctrines, which in the circumstance of the late eighteenth century had millennial dimensions. Iolo Morganwg at the anniversary of the first meeting at Primrose Hill recited an 'Ode on converting a Sword into a Pruning Hook'.[19] More significantly, Iolo made devotion to peace a central aspect of the ceremonial of the Gorsedd.[20] A circle was made of small stones, which was believed to be an ancient custom. Iolo Morganwg called this *Cylch Cyngrair*, the Circle of Concord or of Confederation. In the centre of this circle was the *Maen Gorsedd*, an altar on which was placed a sword, and all the bards assisted in sheathing it. 'The ceremony', so goes the description of the Primrose Hill meeting in 1792, 'was attended with a proclamation, the substance of which was that the *Bards of the Island of Britain* (for such is their ancient title) were the heralds and ministers of peace, and never bore a naked weapon in the presence of anyone: nor was it lawful for any person to bear one, on any pretence, in their presence'. [21]

The most important feature of bardic revivalism was the claim that the bards were descendants of the druids. This fundamentally altered their claims to antiquity, taking the claim for authenticity beyond the minstrels and bards at the courts of the Medieval princes into the mists of time. Iolo Morganwg was the ideologist of this radicalism, but Samwell was a natural supporter of claims for the antiquity of Welsh traditions. Indeed, he may have written the report of the first Primrose Hill Gorsedd which appeared in the *Morning Chronicle*:

> The *Bardic Institution* of the *Ancient Britons*, which is the very same as the *Druidic*, has been from the earliest times, through all ages, to the present day, retained by the *Welch*. Foreign writers, ancient and modern, have fallen into a great mistake, in considering the *Bards* and *Druids* as different orders. . . . *Druidism*, which the *Welch*, rightly calls *bardism*, has been sought for in vain by historians in Greek, Roman and other foreign authors. They are now informed, if they will attend to it, that any regular *Welch Bard* can in a few minutes give them a much better account of it, than all the books in the world; and at the same time the most convincing proofs, that it is now exactly the same that it was two thousand years ago.[22]

If the Welsh were in the process of rediscovering, remaking and repossessing their past, as Rhys Jones has argued, the confidence and casualness of their claim to authenticity would seem to invite caricature. [23] But the claim could be made this way because of the pervasive antiquarianism of the Enlightenment in Britain, which was the sole perquisite neither of radicals nor of the Celtic nations. Thomas Gray shunned fame and devoted much of the latter part of his life to the study of early poetry in English and the Celtic and Scandinavian languages. [24] If such enthusiasm invited ridicule, it would not only be the Welsh who were ridiculed. The willingness to believe in heroic and tragic pasts helps to account for the forgeries of tradition by Macpherson, Chatterton and Iolo Morganwg.

This is not to deny that there was a specifically Welsh dimension to antiquarian radicalism. Bardic imagery had become associated with the Welsh landscape. Picturesque travellers searched in the Conwy valley for the site where the last bard had made his despairing plunge, seeking to match Gray's words with a precise landscape, although Gray had never ventured into the valley. [25] Welshmen, most notably Thomas Pennant, had made distinguished contributions to the literature of travel and to the taste for evoking the past within a picturesque context. None of this was particularly radical, although its context was broadly Whiggish, and it was shaped by and in turn shaped contemporary taste. However, the antiquarian recovery which came from the Welsh endeavour had a more lasting impact than that of their English compatriots. Iolo Morganwg was central to this, and there was certainly no equivalent genius in England. Perhaps William Blake was the nearest, but his challenge to mainstream English culture was marginalized both by the artistic establishment and by political repression. Welsh bards had a much greater plausibility, and Iolo milked this to the utmost, proudly proclaiming that he was a descendant of Oliver Cromwell (was it a coincidence that Samwell believed that he had seen Cromwell's embalmed head? [26]) and that he, along with Evan Evans, was the last representative of the druids. For Iolo the ancient druids had 'breathed the invincible Spirit of Liberty', and he was intent on breathing that spirit into his Welsh contemporaries. [27] Such were his skill, erudition and imagination that it was not until the twentieth century that his complex interweaving of fact and fiction, myth and history would begin to be unravelled.

A further aspect of Welsh claims to an authentic heroic past was the belief that the Welsh prince, Madog ab Owain Gwynedd, had discovered America in the late twelfth century, and that his Welsh-speaking and Christian descendants had survived as the Mandan Tribe amongst the American Indians. The myth had appeared in David Powell's *The Historie of Cambria* (1584), which published Humphrey Llwyd's account of Madog (*c*.1559). This was known to John Dee, polymath of Welsh descent, advisor to Queen Elizabeth I, and an early prophet of empire. He suggested that Madog's discovery enabled Britain to challenge Spanish claims to the New World. It was no coincidence that the myth was revived at a time when Britain had once more gone to war with Spain. In 1740, just after the beginnng of the War of Jenkin's Ear, Revd Theophilus Evans in the second edition of his *Drych y Prif Oesoedd* (1716) (Mirror of the First Ages) retold the tale of Madog, prefacing the account with the story that a Welsh Presbyterian minister from New York, Morgan Jones, had been captured by Indians and had saved his skin by praying in Welsh, whereupon his tongue was recognized and he was reprieved. Jones then spent four months with the Indians, preaching to them regularly in Welsh. The story encouraged imitations, and 'by the 1780s a veritable tide of Welsh Indian stories was breaking on English-speaking America'.[28] They soon reached London and interest in Madoc grew apace, coming to a climax with the publication in 1791 of Revd John Williams's *An enquiry into the truth of the tradition concerning the discovery of America by Prince Madog ab Owen Gwynedd, about the year 1170*, which authenticated the myth. Samwell, who lived in expectation of making new discoveries of the ancient past, had already become convinced of the authenticity of the tale. While serving on the *Crocodile*, the ship had put in at Cork, where he had met Charles Vallancey, an engineer working on the fortifications of the harbour. Vallancey was an antiquarian and philologist who had already published books on the Irish language. He explained to Samwell his thesis that 'many of the Indian Nations in America speak a dialect of Celtic' and that it 'also prevailed in many parts of Asia'. Samwell, who had remarked of the Indians he observed in Nootka Sound that 'their language was remarkably harsh and guttural and many of their Words not to be pronounced by Europeans', nonetheless thought that, in respect of the American Indians 'in a great measure',[29] Vallancey had proved his thesis and that it was 'curious and new, and well worth the attention of the learned'.[30] By the end of the 1780s, when, with the revolutionary events occurring in France almost anything seemed possible, something like a Madog fever ran through the Welsh literati. Iolo Morganwg was quick to forge texts to prove the authenticity of John Williams's claim. There also appeared on the scene 'General' William August Bowles, who claimed to be of Cherokee descent and who confirmed the story that many Indians were Welsh speaking. It was left to William Owen Pughe to argue that the name Bowles gave to them, the Padoucas, was none other than a corruption of 'Madogwys' or 'Madawgwys', the people of Madog. Samwell, who interviewed Bowles, accepted this view and believed that his new evidence placed the Madog story 'beyond all manner of doubt'.[31] Not all agreed, and there followed an extremely lively debate in the Caractacan Society, which, when the dust had settled, Samwell versified in the poem 'The Padouca Hunt', published shortly after his death.[32] In a letter to the society Samwell had admitted that 'the existence of a race of Welsh Indians' appeared extraordinary. From his account of the debate we learn that the key argument he used for suggesting that the extraordinary was true came from his own experiences with Cook's third expedition. Samwell's sojourn in Tahiti seemed unreal but his exploits and those of his fellows among the 'tawney maids' had undoubtedly happened, even if he exaggerated the degree of miscegenation which took place. Indeed, if fantasy were fact in the Pacific, why not in the Atlantic; if Samwell could journey to Kamchatka, why not Madog to America? The debate became very heated and as Samwell conceded, 'We ended deeper in the dark, Than when we first begun'. The only way to decide the matter was to send an expedition to America to find the Padoucas. Iolo Morganwg declared himself prepared to lead but soon pulled out. Instead, the young John Evans set out on a solo quest. He found the Mandan Indians, but they were not Welsh-speaking Padoucans, and he died a disappointed man soon afterwards (1799). By this time Samwell had also died. The Madog legend, however, continued to exercise a fascination over the Welsh imagination. This has been interpreted as part of a Welsh quest to find a place for themselves in the emerging modern world. A heroic past would give them an identifiable future. [33] The confusion of fact with fantasy and fabrication which occurred in the quest had many parallels in Britain and Europe at the time. Rhys Jones has suggested a different parallel, with the nineteenth-century Maori grand fleet literature, which was a response to cultural annihilation. [34] Yet, important as the language and culture were to Samwell, one cannot detect in him a fear of cultural annihilation. Moreover, in moments of reflection, when he could distance himself from the passions of the moment, he maintained a sense of ironic perspective on almost all he did. In 'The Padouca Hunt' he made no attempt to portray himself in an especially favourable light, neither did he exclude the comments of those who thought he was quite wrong, even 'mad'. Conceived of and styled as a heroic poem, it turned into a brilliant squib, replete with an informative and amusing set of notes on his friends and their proceedings.[35]

Samwell was forever looking for new experiences, and extending his imagination and sympathies to those who lived in very different times and places. Wishing to make imaginative connections with the past, his Pacific experiences enhanced his willingness to accept the unusual and to privilege sympathy and imagination over reason and calculation. This made him gullible, as in his swift authentication of Ireland's Shakespearean forgeries, and often led to disappointment. But he remained irrepressible. A letter of 31 December 1781, which he wrote to Gregson from Spithead, tells of his experiences in a self-revealing way:

> Soon after [my arrival here] I mounted my *Hobby-Horse* & like the wandering Jew rambled about through every town and village within 20 miles of this place, and if you ask me for what purpose I cant tell you, but so it is Matt that I have a whimsical propensity in me to see a *strange Town* & that I believe you never knew it before, this odd passion has had possession of me ever since I can remember, in short it is my Hobby Horse & I find great pleasure in riding it – so whenever our ship come to anchor within twenty miles or so of anything that bears the name of a Town (tho' the bigger the better) I am sure to mount and set off as if the Devil was driving me – often times I get somebody to get up behind me but that's a matter of indifference at least it never hinders me from riding by myself – perhaps you'll think that I ramble about in this manner to make myself acquainted with the learned laws & regulations of our Boroughs & Corporations & to learn wisdom from Mayors and Aldermen – no such thing; there never was perhaps a Traveller less curious about these matters than myself, therefore ask me not why I go on these Quixotical Excursions for I can only say it is my *Hobby-Horse* . . .

Samwell's enjoyment lay in his sense of empathy with the past. He wrote this letter shortly after visiting Carisbrooke Castle on the Isle of Wight, where, musing on the captivity of Charles I, he located the window through which the king had tried to escape. Samwell crept though it 'with a sort of religious awe upon me'. Overwhelmed by feelings of sympathy for the 'fate of that unhappy monarch', he called to mind the lines from Charles Churchill's poem, 'Gotham' (1764),

> What tho' thy faults were many & were great
> What tho' they shook the basis of the state!
> In Royalty, secure thy *person* stood,
> And sacred was the Fountain of thy Blood. [36]

Like Churchill, Samwell believed one should 'make allowances for the failings of humanity'.[37] Maybe, too, his willingness to make allowances for the failings of others lay in his sense of his own personal failings. Yet impatience and disappointment combined when he encountered those who failed to share his feelings for the past. At Carisbrooke he met the village schoolmaster and was disgusted to discover that he knew little about the history of the castle. He had felt equally let down the previous year when, on the last lap of its journey home, the *Discovery* put in at Stromness in the Orkneys. Searching for the remains of 'druidical temples', he came across a lone bagpiper, and his 'warm imagination' immediately cast him in the role of a ministrel 'well versed in antiquities'. He turned out to be as ill-informed as the schoolmaster. However, it would have taken more severe disappointments for Samwell to abandon adventuring forth in the hope of new experiences. [38] In 1791, in one of his excursions, this time with Iolo Morganwg riding behind him, he visited the grave of Laurence Sterne and penned a sentimental poem, subsequently published in the *Gentleman's Magazine*. Devoid of wit, it was written by Samwell the pilgrim, rather than Samwell on his hobby horse.[39] Sterne would have enjoyed the irony. Indeed, as someone whose rule of continence was easily overcome by passion, whose sentimentalism contained within it its own contrariety, and whose wit often offended against the rule of propriety, he was, if not a model for Samwell, a kindred spirit. [40] In his *Sentimental Journey* he described perhaps better than anyone else the sort of traveller that was Samwell, when observing,

> What a large volume of adventures may be grasped within this little span of life by him who interests his heart in everything, and who having eyes to see, what time and chance are perpetually holding out to him as he jouneyeth on his way, misses nothing he can *fairly* lay his hands on. [41]

Samwell was a many-sided man: a Welshman, a Briton, a conscientious surgeon, a humanitarian, a poet and a wit, and a sentimental traveller. His character and experiences led him away from simplicities, and from ploughing a single furrow. His sympathy for, but limited commitment to, the cause of the radicals is indicative of the way he shied away from those who viewed life through a single perspective. He is never predictable: he sympathized with the plight of Charles I, and refused to condemn the Duke of Cumberland for butchery when, on one of his many expeditions, he visited the battlefield of Culloden. [42] Samwell's head would pull him one way, his heart another, and through his own rich experiences he could conduct a vigorous and unending internal debate; unending, because he was aware that there were not just two sides to a question, but that there was a plurality of possibilities. If it is true that we are defined by the 'other', then Samwell's self-definition was inevitably more complex than that of his fellows. There was, it is true, an immense market for 'vicarious voyaging', and many of his friends were vicarious voyagers. [43] Yet they had never confronted the other, whether in sybaritic moments in the South Seas, in a sloop with the French firing on them, or in the hardship of coping with the elements. They lacked the perspective of the voyager; maybe they didn't know how lucky they were. Samwell, like them, also voyaged in the imagination and could get carried into places more exotic and fantastic than he had witnessed, but he also knew the real fantasy of truth, which caused him to refuse to make clear distinctions between truth and fancy. Indeed, his love of fancy, exemplified in his love of Sterne, also gave him a special appreciation of otherness. This gave him a sense

of distance from all things, despite the enthusiasms of the moment. For
him, hubris kept common-sense realism at bay, while the wit of the senti-
mentalist tempered the passion of the bard. If, through the multivalencies
of his own experiences, he had a sense of cultural otherness, his humanitarian cosmopolitanism also gave him a real sense of the other as ourselves.[44]
He freely extended his sympathy to those of whom intellectually he disapproved, allowed broad patriotic feeling to overrule narrower sentiments,
and was unconventional in his interpretation of himself as a 'Humanity
Man'.[45]

Voyaging provided the key element of Samwell's sense of himself. The
voyager probed 'eclectically into anything new' and, as Greg Dening has
argued, 'in many ways it was the actual voyaging more than in the discovered substances that excited. It was the experiencing of otherness
rather than the otherness itself.'[46] Samwell's life was a voyage, but it lacked
the coherence of the voyage which gave it so much meaning, Cook's Third
expedition. Without that, voyaging tended to be a form of escapism, of un-
structured fantasy. Probing 'eclectically into anything new' could become
a form of self-destruction. Samwell, despite his moments of self-emasculation
in drink or drugs, never entirely succumbed to this. In common-sense
terms, the rest of his life after the excitement of Cook's voyage was bound
to be an anticlimax. But Samwell continued to have moments of great
excitement in conflict on the sea, in the new ideas and happenings of a
revolutionary age, and especially in the adrenalin rushes of the Welsh
revivalism of the Gwyneddigion and the Caractacan societies and at the
prospect of uncovering a dramatic new perspective on the past. Moreover,
so long as he was serving on the sea, his life was always going to have a
'what next?' character. Constructive voyaging was difficult, but there was
more coherence in his search than he perhaps fully appreciated. In the first
extant letter to Gregson he says, 'Do you take me to be a Don Quixote that
goes about seeking adventure?' He was indeed quixotic. Yet even though
he appeared to be swept along on the tide of immediate experience, his
letters to Gregson indicate a greater insight into himself and his nature
than he often admitted. Samwell died just when he had gained a position
in which he could have reflected in a stable way on his achievements. Had
he been able to do so, he would have seen that although his life appeared
to go rather too often through the roaring forties and the doldrums, he
remained a sentimental traveller, riding his hobby horse through life,
entranced by its passions, emancipated by its whimsy, and always sympathetic
to his fellow human beings.

Notes

1   Gentleman's Magazine, 1798, LXVIII; Part II, 1085; Davies, 'David Samwell: A Further Note', 257.
2   A translation kindly provided by Daniel Huws which tries to capture the essence of the words of Owen Jones (Owain Myfyr): 'os bydd Camp e fydd *ystremp'*. Davies, 'David Samwell (1751–1798), 123.
3   Letter 39, 7 July 1787.
4   The Anglican Church was also the established Church in Wales. Samwell, as the son of a Welsh Clergyman who could not afford to send him to university, would have known of the deleterious situation of the Welsh Church and the widespread criticism of the abuses of preferment. As Geraint Jenkins has noted, 'It was not simply the absenteeism and dilatoriness of alien bishops which infuriated cultural patriots in Wales. Resentment was also growing because they took advantage of their opportunity to deploy their chosen servants – often close relatives – in strategic positions in the church, and deliberately denied preferment to talented and ambitious Welsh curates.' "Horrid and Unintelligible Jargon": The Case of Thomas Bowles', *Welsh History Review*, 15, 1990–1, 494–523, (519). A comprehensive overview of the situation is provided by Eryn M. White's 'The Established Church, Dissent and the Welsh Language', in Jenkins (ed.), *The Welsh Language before the Industrial* Revolution, pp. 235–88.
5   Letter 27, 5 June 1781.
6   British Library, Add MS 15 030, Myvrian MSS, Samwell to Owen Jones, Paris, 23 March 1798, printed in full in Davies, 'David Samwell (1751–1798)', 95–6.
7   In 1791 George Richards published a poem entitled 'The Aboriginal Britons'. An extract was immediately published in the *New Annual Register* (1791), 180–1, under the heading 'Characteristics of liberty in the savage state of this island, its extinction in the early stages of monarchy, and its revival and influence in the present and civilised state of manners'.
8   Richard Price, 'A Discourse on the Love of our Country' (1789), in Thomas (ed.), *Richard Price: Political Writings*, p. 195.
9   Beaglehole, *Journals*, III, pp. 1152–3.
10 Edmund Burke, *Reflections on the Revolution in France*, ed. J. G. A. Pocock (Indianapolis: Hackett Publishing Co., 1987), p. 41. For the definition of platoon, see T. Dyche and W. Pardon, *A New General English Dictionary* (London: Thomas Ware, third edn, 1740).
11 It was a condition of membership of the society that one should reside in London. The society initially celebrated St David's Day with a ball, but in 1777 they decided to have a dinner instead, which was held on 2 March as St David's Day fell on a Sunday. Leathart, *Origins and Progress*, pp.16–17.
12 Letter 48, 16 July 1794. The quotation is from Milton, 'L'Allegro'. See also Letter 27.
13 Letter 51, 8 October 1795.
14 O'Gorman, *Voters, Patrons and Parties*, p. 303. Sir Watkyn Lewes contested Worcester without success on four occasions: 1773, 1774, 1776, 1780. He campaigned on the platform of the Wilkite Society for the Supporters of the Bill of Rights, namely, the reduction of places and pensions, shorter parliaments and

franchise reform. The honour may have been the unhorsing of the carriage of the Leweses and having it drawn by their supporters, a Wilkite practice.

[15] Letter 6, London, 14 September 1774.

[16] Letter 44, 2 July 1792; Letter 49, August 1795; Letter 54, 31 May 1798; NLW MSS 21282E, Letter 449, David Samwell to Iolo Morganwg (10 July 1791?).

[17] The Gorsedd of Bards of the Isle of Britain was invented by Iolo Morganwg. Prys Morgan has noted that, although the Primrose Hill location was suggested by meetings of the Ancient Druid Order, founded early in that century, the 'gorsedd was an entirely separate association for supporters of all things Welsh, its rites and rituals'. The Gorsedd became associated with the eisteddfod at the Carmarthen eisteddfod in 1819. See Prys Morgan, 'Edward Williams', in H. C. G. Matthew and B. Robinson (eds), *Oxford Dictionary of National Biography* (Oxford: Oxford University Press, 2004).

[18] Davies, 'David Samwell', 101.

[19] Davies, 'David Samwell', 101, n.3.

[20] Iolo distanced his idea of the bardic tradition from that of Gray and others, for he stressed its pacific characteristics. Prys Morgan, *Iolo Morganwg* (Cardiff: University of Wales Press, 1975).

[21] Davies, 'David Samwell', 100.

[22] Davies, 'David Samwell', 99–101.

[23] Rhys Jones, 'Sylwadau Cyfrodor ar Gôr y Cewri; or a British Aboriginal's land claim to Stonehenge', in Christopher Chippindale et al., *Who Owns Stonehenge?* (London: Batsford, 1990), pp. 62–87.

[24] The only translation of Welsh poetry which Gray published also emphasized heroic resistance: 'The Triumph of Owen. A Fragment. From Mr Evans's Specimens of the Welch Poetry; London, 1764'. The Thomas Gray Archive: *www.thomasgray.org*.

[25] Peter Lord, *Clarence Whaite and the Welsh Art World. The Betwys-y-coed Artists' Colony, 1844–1914* (Cardiff: National Library of Wales, 1998), pp. 20–1.

[26] Letter 4, 24 March 1774. Cromwell's body was embalmed on his death. At the Restoration it was exhumed, and his head was placed on a pole and publicly displayed at Westminster Hall. Subsequently there was some controversy as to whether the body dug up was that of Cromwell. The episode is treated in scrupulous detail by H. F. McMains. He argues that the exhumation of Cromwell's body occurred, but that his body was replaced by a more recent corpse before it went through the ritual humiliations, including the displaying of the head. Samwell, it appears, saw the substitute head. H. F. McMains, *The Death of Cromwell* (Lexington: University of Kentucky Press, 2000), pp. 140–78. I would like to thank Professor Michael Bennett for drawing my attention to this study.

[27] Geraint H. Jenkins, 'The cultural uses of the Welsh language', in Jenkins (ed.), *The Welsh Language before the Industrial Revolution*, pp. 369–406 (p. 403).

[28] Williams, *Madoc*, p. 87.

[29] Beaglehole, *Journals*, pp. 1103–4. Williams (Madoc, pp. 2–3) suggests that Samwell was in great demand in the 1780s for his stories of Nootka, but it is unlikely that he distorted his own experience to enhance the myth of Madoc. Williams is on surer ground in pointing to the crisis between Britain and Spain

over Nootka Sound as an important element in the Madog hysteria of the 1790s.

30   BL Ad MS 15030, Myvrian MSS, f.123, Dafydd Ddu to Myfyr (Owen Jones), 18 December 1781. The writings of Charles Vallancey (1721–1812) ranged from works on fortifications and upon tanning to those on linguistics and antiquarian subjects. In 1781 he had just published the second edition of his *A Grammar of the Iberno-Celtic, or Irish language: To which is prefixed, an essay on the Celtic language: shewing the importance of the Iberno-Celtic or Irish dialect, to students in history, antiquity, and the Greek and Roman classics* (Dublin), and presumably this was one of the publications he gave to Samwell.

31   Davies, 'David Samwell's Poem – "The Padouca Hunt"', citing BM Add. MS 14957, Samwell to the Gwyneddigion, 23 March 1791.

32   The Caractacan or Caradogion Society was a debating society founded in 1790 with radical associations with ancient British virtue. Non-Welsh speakers were allowed to attend and debates were in English. It did not survive the repressive legislation of the late 1790s and folded in 1798. Bowen, *David Samwell (Dafydd Ddu Feddyg) 1751–1798*, pp. 79–83.

33   See Morgan, *The Eighteenth Century Renaissance*, ch. 4, 'The Invention of Welshness', pp. 212–22.

34   'Fathering the Pacific: A Putative View', unpublished paper which the author kindly gave me.

35   National Library of Wales MSS 21282E, Letter 449, Samwell to Iolo Morganwg, 10 July 1791.

36   Letter 29, 31 December 1781; Churchill's poem 'Gotham' (1764) concludes with an exposition of Patriot King ideas. Gotham on becoming king would cultivate virtue, stand up to scheming ministers, banish favourites and reward merit. He would govern according to the norms of reason and justice. These were close to Wilkite ideas – Churchill (1731–64) collaborated closely with Wilkes – yet so anodyne that anyone who claimed to be on the side of virtue would accede to them. Douglas Grant (ed.), *The Poetical Works of Charles Churchill* (Oxford: Oxford University Press, 1956), 'Gotham a Poem', Bk II, p. 323, 329–33; Bk. III, pp. 331–48, esp. lines 37–46, 67–102, 505–664.

37   Letter 29, 31 December 1781; Samwell had a good deal in common with Churchill: he was a wit and satirist, with radical sympathies and broad humanitarian sentiments, whose irregular personal life led him to an early grave. Also, Andrew Kippis provided Churchill with some literary employment and was the first to memorialize him, in his *Biographia Britannica*. Thomas Lockwood, *Post-Augustan Satire: Charles Churchill and Satirical Poetry, 1750–1800* (Seattle: University of Washington Press, 1979), p. 142.

38   Letter 29, 31 December 1781; cf. Laurence Sterne, *The Life and Opinions of Tristram Shandy* (1759–67), ed. Graham Petrie, intro. Christopher Ricks (Harmondsworth: Penguin, 1985), vol. I, ch. 7, p. 43: 'Sir, have not the wisest of men in all ages, not excepting Solomon himself, – have they not had their HOBBY-HORSES; –their running horses, – their coins and their cockle shells, their drums and their trumpets, their fiddles, their pallets, – their maggots and their butterflies? – and so long as a man rides his HOBBY-HORSE peaceably and quietly along the King's highway, and neither compels you or me to get up

behind him, – pray, Sir, what have either you or I to do with it?'

39   Davies 'David Samwell', p. 115; the poem was printed twice, a shorter version
      in 1791 and a longer one in 1792. Sterne was buried on 22 March 1768 in St.
      George's burial ground in Bayswater Road. According to a story believed to
      be authentic, his body was dug up two days later and sold for dissection.
      Only later was a headstone put in place near the site of his grave, through the
      philanthropy of two admirers. Samwell either did not know this story, or he
      preferred to make no reference to it.

40   R. F. Brissenden, *Virtue in Distress: Studies in the Novel of Sentiment from
      Richardson to Sade* (London: Macmillan, 1974), p. 36, notes that Sterne was a
      member of a society of Demoniacs whose conversation 'if nothing else, was
      Rabelaisian'. He also points out that: 'Sexual libertinism . . . is the physical
      expression of a sceptical and critical attitude to life, an attitude which, if taken
      to extremes, becomes anarchic and nihilistic.' These elements and possibilities
      were present in Samwell's life. They also mark him off from the tradition which
      Seward represented. See John Brewer, *The Pleasures of the Imagination: English
      Culture in the Eighteenth Century* (London: HarperCollins, 1997), pp. 573–612.

41   Laurence Sterne, *A Sentimental Journey* (1768), Graham Petrie (ed.), intro. by
      A. Alvarez (Harmondsworth: Penguin, 1986), p. 51.

42   Letter 37, 16 September 1784.

43   Dening, 'The Theatricality of Observing', p. 453.

44   For these reflections I am indebted to Greg Dening, *Performances* (Carlton
      South: Melbourne University Press, 1996), pp. 155–6.

45   He used the expression in relation to his opposition to the slave trade, but in
      other respects he was a far from consistent reformer; Letter 41, 11 October
      1788. Typically, he described Paine as 'our Shakespeare in politics', but never
      wished 'to see his politics enforced'; Letter 49, 9 August 1795.

46   Dening, 'The Theatricality of Observing', p. 453.

3

David Samwell: Pacific ethnographer and historian

NICHOLAS THOMAS

Captain James Cook's second voyage of 1772–75 had explored the south
Pacific far more extensively than any previous navigation. It had established
finally that there was no southern continent, it had revisited a number of
tropical Pacific islands already known to Europeans and it had located
many new ones. If its central geographic finding was negative, the
completeness of its accomplishment was unprecedented, and the variety
of its human and natural historical observation astonishing. By mid–1775
it had been decided that a further voyage would take place. One was
needed to repatriate the famous Pacific Islander Mai (known generally as
Omai in England), who had been brought home by Tobias Furneaux, the
captain of Cook's consort, the *Adventure*. It was initially proposed that
this expedition would be under the command of Cook's lieutenant, Charles
Clerke. But Cook in the end disdained retirement, not least because the
third voyage would, like its predecessors, have major geographic ambitions,
as well as a humanitarian duty. There was another object of long-standing
navigational speculation that was potentially as important for trade as a
southern continent might have been. Admiralty lords, merchants and the
'closet philosophers' of the Royal Society all wondered whether there was
a navigable north-west passage that would permit a quick route from
Europe to the Pacific, and specifically to the ports of east Asia.[1]

There had been dozens of attempts to locate a passage from the Atlantic
side. None had succeeded, but interest remained intense. In the 1770s,
speculation began with the thesis that ice formed from rivers, not in open
sea; there might therefore be open water and a route across the North
Pole itself. But in any case the coasts of north America were scarcely
charted, and straits might exist that had not yet been found. A parliamentary prize was offered, and a plan was devised that in effect inverted
Cook's strategy in the southern oceans. Exploratory forays would be
made during the warmer months over one or two successive summers.
During the intervening periods the ships could be refitted and resupplied
in the tropics, which themselves might be further explored. The exploration

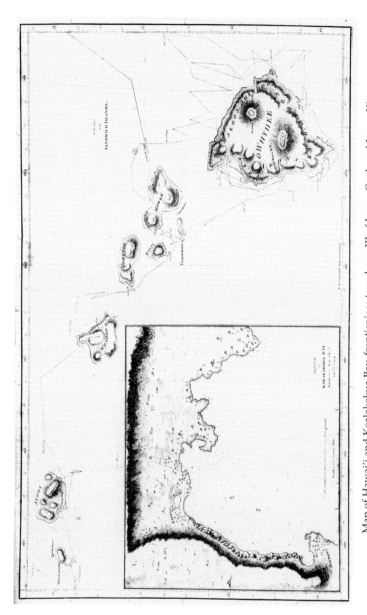

Map of Hawai'i and Kealakekua Bay, frontispiece to volume III of James Cook and James King, *A Voyage to the Pacific Ocean,* 1784.

itself would involve tracing the western coast of America northward, while probing apparent openings for a passage through the continent that would lead into Hudson's or Baffin Bay. [2] The *Resolution* and *Discovery* left Britain in the summer of 1776 and would return just over four years later. Their findings on the key geographic issue would again be negative: the north American continent was indeed a continent, in fact one that extended much further west, toward Asia, than had previously been understood; it seemed that there was no channel through it, and the observations of ice fields to the north of Bering Strait placed it beyond doubt that ice was formed at sea. Even in midsummer, the ice field did not retreat to a degree that permitted a ship to sail either east above America or west above Asia toward the north Atlantic.

The third voyage's accomplishment in mapping the Pacific coasts of north America was, however, eclipsed: above all by the tragic drama of Cook's death on the newly discovered island of Hawai'i, but secondarily by the degree to which much of the interest of the voyage again lay in encounters with the cultures of Pacific islanders. Delays early in the voyage meant that the first attempt to reach northern waters had to be postponed from the summer of 1777 to that of 1778: as a result, the whole of 1777 was occupied in calling at Tasmania, New Zealand, Tonga and the Society Islands, among other places; Hawaiians were encountered for the first time at Kauai in early 1778. The voyage was, therefore, made up above all of human contacts and conflicts. The contacts were with people who were, from the European point of view, novel, curious and exotic; relationships with them were marked by ups and downs, by benevolent mutual hospitality, by damaging sexual contacts and by violence. The narration of the voyage was therefore replete with matter of interest, but also matter that was morally problematic and controversial. The excitement of novel encounters and the problems of their morality are vividly present in the writings of the surgeon David Samwell.

In the preface to his *Voyage Round the World*, an engaging narrative of Cook's second expedition, George Forster sought to justify what he rightly anticipated would be a contentious book. Cook's own account, he argued, would inevitably reflect the commander's preoccupation with the practical requisites of the voyage and with matters maritime, while his own ranged far more widely than 'the proper field of the navigator', and profited from the many opportunities that he had had to examine 'the manifold objects which Nature had scattered' throughout the lands visited, notably including the varieties of people encountered in the Pacific islands. [3] In the written records of Cook's three voyages, the writings of natural historians and others indeed complement the officers' logs, and Cook's own journals, in vitally informative ways. For the first voyage, the journal of Joseph Banks is rich, quirky and engaging for its responses to Tahitian and Maori culture and society. For the second, Johann Reinhold Forster's, that became the basis of George Forster's published account, is wide-ranging, nuanced and humanistic. The artist Parkinson, the surgeon Monkhouse, and the astronomer Wales likewise left crucial information that – whatever its biases and limitations – does much to extend under-standings of Pacific cultures and their early cross-cultural encounters.

The ethnographic record from Cook's third voyage of 1776–80 was richer still. Cook's own interest in Polynesian custom had deepened, and he would write more extensively about indigenous rituals than he ever had before. In Tonga, where he admired the people, his curiosity was particularly rapacious. Other seamen were more aware than before of the unprecedented accomplishment of the voyages and level of public interest in their findings. More were prompted to write more extensively, and more was published after this voyage than after either of its predecessors. Yet the two richest narratives, after Cook's own, did not appear in print until the 1960s, when J. C. Beaglehole included them in his edition of Cook's journals. These were both the journals of surgeons. William Anderson, born about 1748, was surgeon on the *Resolution*, while David Samwell was surgeon's mate on that ship until Anderson's death in August 1778. In conformity with rank order, Anderson was replaced by John Law, who moved across from the consort, the *Discovery*, while Samwell in turn took Law's place on that vessel.

Anderson had been surgeon's mate on the second voyage, in the course of which he composed some sort of voyage narrative that does not survive. He quarrelled with the Forsters – we are often told that they fell out sooner or later with everyone – but at the same time evidently absorbed a great deal from them, as is reflected in the wide-ranging attention to natural history in his third-voyage journal, in remarks on the effects of climate, and in his animated descriptions of indigenous culture. Tongan dance, for example, struck many voyage participants as perfect in its timing, elegance and regularity; Anderson's description of the performances wit-nessed in May and June 1777 is minute and exemplary, by the standards of anthropological reporting of the period.

David Samwell's journal is quite different. It springs from a wide-ranging, intellectually vigorous imagination, but lacks the specific natural-historical framing of Anderson's record. The strength of Samwell's narrative is its attention to human interaction, and particularly its free expression of Samwell's own responses to particular peoples and situations. Samwell is notorious for the frankness of his reference to the sexual pleasures of the voyage, but this is not so much an indication of any atypical preoccupation – Cook was just about alone in refraining from sexual contacts – as consistent with the engaged and candid quality of his writing. This comes through, irrespective of whether men or women, European or indigenous, are discussed, enthusiastically or disparagingly. His observations after a fleeting visit to Atiu, never before called at by Europeans, are brief but representative. Anderson, John Gore and Mai ('Omai') had ventured ashore through surf, but had been prevented by people from freely exploring, and were more troubled by a sense that people would not let them leave.

> Our People were apprehensive that the Indians intended to keep them on the Island, & perhaps the sight of the Powder & description of their Arms which they had seen in the Boats made them alter their Intentions. Still it is probable that the Natives intended only to keep them in durance for a short time merely to gratify their Curiosity, for they were as much pleased & astonished with looking at them as the rabble rout in England are with seeing a Collection of wild Beasts at a Country Fair.
>
> They are a stout good looking People. Some of them have their Bodies tattawed in various places, but most of them only their Legs which makes them appear at a distance as if booted, they wear a piece of Cloth variously striped round their middle & have Sandals on their Feet. Some of the Chiefs are amazingly corpulent. Their tattawing seems to be a kind of Heraldry, for those of the same tribe or Family were marked exactly alike, however our stay was too short to make us certain of such Circumstances as these. The Natives call the Island *Watdu*, it is situated in Lat. 20.00 S, Long. 202.00 E, it was never visited before by Europeans . . . The first Question that was put to us by these People & those of the last Island was, 'Who is your Are or Chief?'[4]

Samwell exhibits prejudices typical of observers of the period: it is natural to him to make a comparison between a group of Polynesians and 'the rabble rout in England'. Yet he makes the observation in order to suggest that the coercive, perhaps threatening acts of these people were motivated merely by curiosity – we might add, by their reciprocation of the voyagers' own inquisitiveness. He makes a useful observation of the use of footwear – that was generally rare in the Pacific, and here responded to the difficulty of walking on the extensive coral fringing reefs. He tells us a little about local tattoos, and interprets them as 'a kind of Heraldry' which is inadequate but not totally misleading. Some motifs were, it is now thought, associated with particular genealogies; some served rather to mark the followers of a certain chief. He acknowledges in any case that the visit was too short to obtain conclusive information on the matter and concludes his brief reflections by recording the question asked of the visitors, which gives some sense of what was central to Islanders' understandings of peoples and societies.

Samwell's observations are generally far less abbreviated than this, and they range over the appearance of country, flora and fauna, but emphasize the qualities and doings of people: the physique, ornamentation, dress and disposition of Islanders ('Their Arms & Cheek bones are also marked in memory of the Dead'); their implements, their subsistence, their boats, their houses, and their arts and music ('Their carving they execute very neat, this art is chiefly employed by them in ornamenting their Clubs, which they carve all over with the shape of Men, Birds, Dogs & Fish &c. in different parts').[5] Although he did make sustained inquiries, and his linguistic and literary interests are manifest in the fact that he made the first serious transcriptions of Maori songs, his comments are more often immediate, responding to what he has just seen or what has just taken place. His reflections are accordingly diverse and sometimes inconsistent; in contrast to the Forsters, he tends not to attempt to integrate them into an anthropological or geographical theory. He makes remarks, but he does not make systematic assessments of particular peoples, nor does he generally rank or assess one set of islanders relative to another.

There are exceptions to this characterization. One of the richest phases of the voyage was the encounter with the Tongans. Cook and others who had participated in the second voyage knew the people of Eua and Tongatapu from a five-day visit in 1773 and those of Nomuka from an even shorter anchorage in 1774. Impressions of the people, who were clearly related to the Tahitians but somewhat distinct, were favourable, and Cook named the group the Friendly Islands. During the third voyage, the objective of reaching the American north-west coast had to be deferred from the northern summer of 1777 to that of 1778; hence, available time and the need for provisions made a considerably more extended stay desirable. In the event, two and a half months were spent visiting the main islands of the archipelago and in extensive trade. Objects were continually appropriated from the ships, and the mariners took increasingly punitive measures against those they took to be thieves, but relationships with the chiefs were for the most part marked by extensive mutual hospitality (though later sources indicate that serious consideration was given to killing the Europeans in order to seize the ships). Cook's admiration for the level of social stratification, and the elaborate deference shown to the paramount chief, Paulaho, was marked.

It is interesting that Samwell saw the polity very differently. The Europeans had generally met with friendliness, he noted, which attested to the hospitable temperament of the Tongans in general. But the common people were subjected to 'barbarous Treatment', which sprang, not from any national disposition, but from an aspect of government, namely 'the exorbitant Power of the Chiefs'. This power extended, he understood, to the capacity to put a man to death on a whim. He conceded that 'our scanty knowledge of their Language' and, again, the brevity of the visit made it unlikely that government could be fully understood. He nevertheless speculated that the laws regulated the conduct of one chief relative to another, 'but that the common People are intirely at their [the chiefs'] Disposal in respect both to their Lives & Property: of the latter it may be doubted whether they have any!'[6] Samwell was at once correct in grasping that Tongan chiefs had far more power than, say, senior men among the Maori of New Zealand, the other Polynesians whom he had had, at this point of the voyage, the best opportunity to observe. His hunch that commoners lacked property was more or less right, though neither he nor any other eighteenth–century visitor would understand the imbrication of Tongan ritual sovereignty, titular ownership and actual use rights.[7] But even if he had had greater insight into the customary bases of these political hierarchies, one suspects that Samwell's radical temperament would still have prompted him to lament the inequalities here.

Samwell's rich journal – which runs to over 140,000 words – was not published in itself, nor was it drawn upon by Canon John Douglas in his editorial work on the official publication, *Voyage to the Pacific Ocean*, that appeared finally in 1784. But if Samwell's account of the voyage as a whole did not reach a public, his narrative of its most notorious moment would be tremendously influential. Samwell does not appear to have been as close to Cook as Anderson was, but Samwell certainly admired Cook very deeply, and responded to his death by inquiring into the circumstances as fully as he could, resulting in a careful and extended section of his journal. As is explained elsewhere, he worked this up as part of the *Biographia Britannica* entry for Andrew Kippis, and then published it separately in the pamphlet that is reproduced here. Kippis in turn wrote the first full biography of Cook – in fact essentially an abridgement of the three published voyage narratives, preceded by an abbreviated account of Cook's career to 1768 – and relied substantially on Samwell for the account of the hero's death. Most nineteenth–century Cook biographies were rehashes of Kippis's, hence this version of events received, albeit in adapted form, remarkably wide circulation for well over a century.[8]

The Hawaiian islands were unknown to Europeans until Cook's third voyage (though some believe that undocumented Spanish contact may have taken place before then). In January 1778, en route from the Society Islands to America, the *Resolution* and *Discovery* sighted the islands of Oahu, Kauai and Niihau, and made contact with people who – affinities of language, society, tattooing and material culture told them – were evidently related to the Polynesians they had already met in Tahiti, Tonga, New Zealand and elsewhere. This visit was short: Cook could afford to lose no time in reaching America. But brief impressions and Cook's prior Pacific experience suggested that good anchorages might be found in these islands, and supplies of pigs and vegetables readily obtained. Later in the year, after tracing the American coast north around Alaska, touching at Siberia and investigating the Bering Sea, he therefore judged that the 'Sandwich Islands' (the group had been named after the first Lord of the Admiralty) would provide a good base for winter refreshment, and could at the same time be properly charted.

Cook's intuition was that the group extended well to the east of the islands he had seen earlier in the year. He therefore sailed not back to Kauai, but into what could well have been open water hundreds of miles to the east; yet the sighting of Maui in late November 1778 proved him right. A week later, after a good deal of barter with people who came off in canoes, the ships moved to windward (eastward) of Maui and came in sight of the great island of Hawai'i itself, that spectacularly featured snow-covered mountains and active volcanoes. For some weeks Cook coasted the island without seeking an anchorage, in part because he sought to regulate trade and in part because he wanted to restrain sexual contacts between his crew and local women: throughout the voyage he had been disturbed and angered by the impact of venereal diseases upon pre-viously unexposed populations. His men were in the frustrating situation of seeing, but being unable to visit, an apparently beautiful and opulent land. Finally, on 17 January 1779, the ships came to anchor in Kealakekua Bay, a broad opening on the south-western coast of Hawai'i. While Cook's ships had, on a number of occasions, been greeted by curious and enthusiastic crowds in Tahiti and elsewhere, nothing prepared them for the scale of this welcome: the bay was crowded with great canoes, its foreshores with people, perhaps 10,000, Lieutenant James King thought. Cook and some associates landed, and Cook was immediately made a participant in a series of rites on the *heiau* or temple of Hikiau, located at the southern edge of the bay. For several weeks the British enjoyed an extraordinary degree of hospitality. Somewhat puzzlingly, the Hawaiian king, Kalaniopu'u, did not appear until 25 January, but from this point onward made Cook a series of gifts of great value – including sacred feather cloaks, among the emblems of divine royalty – and received the most prestigious trade goods that Cook could offer in return. By early February, the ships were well supplied, and preparations were made to depart. The Hawaiian chiefs now wanted to know when the British would leave, and were pleased that it would be soon. On 4 February the ships unmoored and sailed away, intending to explore the remainder of the archipelago, but then were caught in storms. A mast was damaged, and Cook judged that he had to return to Kealakekua, since they had not sighted earlier any good anchorage on any other island.

On 11 February, the *Resolution* and *Discovery* again reached Kealakekua, and the mariners were struck immediately by the lack of any welcome. The Islanders seemed cool; though some trade was resumed, they were 'troublesome' and 'insolent'; sailors on shore trying to fill water casks were harassed; things were stolen, and relationships deteriorated rapidly. On the afternoon of 13 February, a boat's party attempting to seize a man and a canoe (implicated in a theft) were stoned and beaten; without the intervention of a chief Palea, they might well have been killed. On the morning of 14 February, it was found that the *Discovery*'s cutter had been taken from a mooring. Cook went ashore with a party of marines, planning to take Kalaniopu'u hostage against the boat's return; at the same time, he sent boats out to prevent canoes leaving the bay, thinking also of im-pounding them. At Tahiti, Raiatea and Tonga, Cook had on previous occasions seized people of high rank in response to theft or to the desertion of his own men. These actions had produced anger and trauma among Islanders, but in each case succeeded in having his property or men brought back. On this occasion – as Samwell describes – the attempt collapsed into chaos. The king, at first willing, then was entreated not to go, and would not approach Cook's boat. News arrived that a chief had been killed on the other side of the bay. Insults were traded, and violence flared, leaving Cook, four of his men and an unknown number of Hawaiians dead. [9]

This event has been perennially contentious. It was made clear in the published 1784 *Voyage* that Cook was treated with a sort of adoration by the Hawaiians, and the poet William Cowper, among other readers, con-sidered that he had allowed himself to be worshipped, and therefore incurred divine wrath. [10] This theme was taken up by the American missionaries in nineteenth–century Hawai'i, who lambasted Cook's complicity in native idolatry, while drawing attention to incidents of cruelty and violence perpetrated by the mariners, and promulgating a Hawaiian tradition that Cook had had sex with a 'princess', to whom he had com-municated venereal disease. (The tradition expresses a conventional aspect of exchange with a person considered as a visiting chief of high rank, but in a literal sense is almost certainly untrue.) Though evangelically motivated, this critique, which implied that Cook's death derived from his own misconduct and aggression, carried over to secular and anti-imperial commentary, such as Mark Twain's late nineteenth–century Hawaiian travelogue. [11] On the other hand, Cook was consistently idealized in Britain and in the settler nations of Canada, New Zealand and Australia, where he was presented as a 'humane conquistador'. From this side, the initially ambivalent representation of Hawaiians as noble savages who had killed Cook in tragic circumstances was replaced during the nineteenth century by a more conventional colonialist denigration. [12]

More recently, a parallel controversy attracted unusually wide attention. In *The Apotheosis of Captain Cook*, Gananath Obeyesekere attacked Marshall Sahlins's influential historical-structuralist interpretation of Cook's death. Concerned to transcend the opposition between history and structure that had distinguished the classic Lévi-Straussian anthropological paradigm, Sahlins had argued, in a series of publications from the late 1970s and 1980s, that event and structure could be understood as dynamically related. His central example was Cook's death, and he argued that this event was shaped by the basic structures of the Hawaiian culture and polity, and specifically by the opposition between the conquering god of war, Ku, who was closely identified with the ruling kings, and the god of peace and agriculture, Lono, associated with people of the land or commoners. The Hawaiian calendar was organized around a ritual cycle in which Lono was pre-eminent for a period of horticultural rites known as the Makahiki, during which war was taboo, and Ku and his representatives, including the king himself, went into seclusion. During this time, the priests of Lono conducted rituals; toward the end of the cycle Lono withdrew, and Ku and the king resumed their pre-eminence.

While it was recorded in the voyage sources that Cook had indeed been routinely addressed as Lono, and noted by the historian Gavan Daws that the timing was fortuitous – Cook appeared around the beginning of the Makahiki – Sahlins ingeniously demonstrated that many aspects of his circuit of the island and visit corresponded, or were made by the Hawaiians to correspond, with Makahiki ritual. This also accounted for the change in the Hawaiian disposition. Cook went away about the time he should have, but was unwelcome on his return. Whatever confrontation provided the immediate cause of violence and of his death, by mid February the odds were structurally weighted against him. Obeyesekere was not hostile to Sahlins's theory, but was offended by the claim that an indigenous people should regard a visiting European as a god. This was, he considered, little more than a piece of colonial myth-making that Sahlins had dignified, and a smokescreen that obscured the immediate and actual causes of Cook's death. These, Obeyesekere claimed, derived from the explorer's fatigue, irrationality and increasing violence. The killing was an act of rational resistance to aggression, not the upshot of any identification with a native deity, he attempted to demonstrate. [13]

The course of this debate has been much reviewed and need not be retraced here. The point of interest is that an emphasis on Cook's violence, of the sort recently enlarged upon by Obeyesekere, dates back to the immediate aftermath. Those on board the *Resolution* and *Discovery* mostly agreed, as they debated what had happened later in the day on 14 February, and on succeeding days, that the Hawaiian action had not been pre-meditated. But some, including Cook's second-in-command and successor, Charles Clerke, thought that fighting and fatality could have been averted, and that it was Cook's action, in firing at a man who was throwing a stone or perhaps merely a piece of breadfruit, that triggered the escalation of the situation. Others thought precisely the reverse, that Cook's commit-ment to avoid taking the lives of Islanders allowed him to dither, or prevented him from taking forceful action earlier. It was asserted that as he withdrew towards his boat, he made the mistake of turning his back to the Hawaiians, in order to signal to the men in the boats that they should cease firing upon the people, and that it was this that was fatal to him. Both sides imagined an error of judgement on Cook's part, one of excessive anger and the other of excessive humanity.

Lieutenant James King had great regard for Cook, but knew that his temper was prone to flare, and seems to have shared Clerke's judgement that some hasty violence on Cook's part caused the tense situation to explode. However, neither he nor Clerke had been on the spot – the former was on shore, on the southern, opposite side of the bay, while the latter was on board the *Discovery*. It was found, when the accounts of the miserably confused scene were gathered and reviewed, that the sailors and marines disagreed about many points, and some were said to change their minds, as discussion progressed. The only written account by an eyewitness was that of Lieutenant Molesworth Phillips, who commanded the marines. Phillips's manuscript is not known to survive, but it appears to have been closely transcribed by Charles Clerke in his journal. Phillips reported that after it became apparent that Kalaniopu'u could not be induced to enter a British boat, Cook gave up the thought of taking him, and was about to embark when challenged by a warrior with an iron spike or dagger, ob-tained in trade from the British. This man appeared poised to throw a stone at Cook, and Cook fired small shot at him, but the man was wearing a heavy battle-mat, a form of native armour, and the pellets accordingly – Phillips judged – had 'no other effect than farther to provoke and encourage them'. It was this shot of Cook's that, Clerke considered, had exacerbated the situation beyond a tenable point. Phillips himself does not make it clear whether he believed that Cook needed to fire, or should have fired, at this point; nor whether he might have ignored the man, and embarked himself and his party safely.

Considerable emphasis has been placed upon this point by subsequent commentators. Beaglehole, for example, considers that Cook 'snapped' at this vital moment, that this snapping resulted from his exhaustion, and that the Cook of a few years earlier might rather have acted with greater care and restraint, that the tragedy might hence have been avoided. [14] Cook's action certainly fuelled the tension but it does not follow that violence would have been avoided, had he not fired. Other accounts suggest that the news of the killing of the chief Kaulima by men in one of the boats across the bay arrived at this moment, and triggered a wave of anger. It needs also to be considered that Cook was simply going too far, in attempting to take a Hawaiian king hostage: especially in the context of the waning of Lono's status and authority after the conclusion of the Makahiki, this represented an intolerable challenge to the Hawaiian order. Hence the question of whether Cook was fatally aggressive at this critical moment is not so much unresolvable as misconceived: the causes of violence lay not in the immediate circumstances but in a confrontation that had a number of layers.

Back in London, the Hawaiian meanings and distinctions that made up a number of these layers would be invisible, as the voyage narrative was edited for official publication. James King was given the task of writing the continuation of Cook's own journal, which broke off at the point of the first arrival at Kealakekua Bay. This would mean that the first two volumes were Cook's and the third King's. This third volume opened dramatically with the account of the stay at Hawaii, and of Cook's death. When he composed the latter, King was clearly mindful of the confusion and contradiction present in the eyewitness accounts. He followed the only written eyewitness testimony, that of Phillips, and was understandably equivocal in his account of the final fatal moments.

> Our unfortunate Commander, the last time he was seen distinctly, was standing at the water's edge, and calling out to the boats to cease firing, and to pull in. If it be true, as some of those who were present have imagined, that the marines and boat-men were firing without his orders, and that he was desirous of preventing any further bloodshed, it is not improbable, that his humanity, on this occasion, proved fatal to him. For it was remarked, that whilst he faced the natives, none of them had offered any violence, but that having turned about, to give his orders to the boats, he was stabbed in the back, and fell with his face into the water. [15]

The phrasing here seems intended to air but not support what 'some of those who were present' imagined. King proceeds to insert a sketch of Cook's life and character, and writes a few pages later that: 'His temper might perhaps have been blamed, as subject to hastiness and passion, had not these been disarmed by a disposition the most benevolent and humane.'[16] The positive qualification – which eighteenth–century readers could easily have put down to politeness – carries less weight than the admission that precedes it. It is perhaps surprising that an official publication dedicated to the voyage of a dead hero even went so far as to acknowledge that the hero had a hasty temper, but it is consistent with King's apparently genuine concern to provide a full and true account.

The beginning of David Samwell's pamphlet, *The Death of Captain Cook*, implies that people did read between the lines of the official *Voyage* in precisely this way. 'Public opinion seemed to attribute the loss of Captain Cook's life, in some measure, to rashness or too much confidence on his side; whereas nothing can be more ill-founded or unjust.' The account that follows is clearly intended to vindicate Cook. It emphasizes that the mission to take Kalaniopu'u hostage was, as far as anyone could anticipate, prudently planned and not at all rash; it suggests that, once it became apparent that the king could not be taken captive, Cook acted essentially defensively. But if Samwell had an argument, his effort to reconstruct the confusing moments of violence was nevertheless rigorous and searching. He clearly talked to as many people as he possibly could and made efforts to sift their stories. His version of events adds a good deal to Phillips's report, and mentions in particular the crucial detail that Phillips omitted. In all likelihood, the news of Kaulima's death explains the decisive shift in the feeling of the Hawaiian crowd, and that precipitated the outbreak of aggression.

Samwell provides a blow-by-blow account of the fracas involving Palea and the boat's crew, which took place during the afternoon preceding Cook's death, and mentions in passing that at the same time Cook was also in pursuit of the thief, on foot, apparently wilfully misdirected by Hawaiians, on the shores and foothills to the south of Kealakekua Bay. He does not report that Cook seems to have been angered, as he commonly was, by the thief's 'insolence', and determined to punish him in some way. His failure to do so perhaps left him in a state of resentment, and – some commentators have supposed – caused him to be irrationally angry the following morning.[17] Yet even those who saw Cook's temper as a cause of the violence that later occurred do not say that he took his boats across to Ka'awaloa in a rage. It is this point, in any case, that Samwell is precisely concerned to deny.

Samwell's account is generally consistent with that of Phillips and with other testimony, though there are many minor inconsistencies that cannot now be adjudicated. In one significant respect it is likely to be distorted by Samwell's propensity to idealize Cook. Phillips indicates that after Cook ineffectively shot at the man protected by the battle-mat, after Phillips was attacked by a chief, after stones were thrown and a marine knocked down, a 'general attack' began and Cook 'gave orders to the Marines to fire'. According to Samwell, when the Hawaiians stoned the marines they:

> without waiting for orders, returned it with a general discharge of musketry, which was instantly followed by a fire from the boats. At this Captain Cook was heard to express his astonishment: he waved his hand to the boats, called to them to cease firing, and to come nearer in to receive the marines. [18]

This is, of course, the version of events that King reported but doubted. It was given memorable visual expression by John Webber in his grand *Death of Captain Cook*, which transformed the mere wave into a forthright humanitarian signal to cease fire. Webber's gesture was certainly invented. Phillips's and Samwell's versions of events might almost be reconciled, if Cook did in fact order those marines on shore (as distinct from the men in the boats) to fire. In all likelihood he did so, since the threat to his life and that of his men was now manifest, and he had fired himself before, and ordered fire, under such circumstances. Yet he may not have expected the boat's crews to join the fire; those men could not row and shoot at the same time, and he might rather have hoped that they were doing the former, in order to bring the boats up to the shore, so that those whose situation be-came desperate could get away. In hindsight, Cook would certainly have regretted the killing of Hawaiians – he had regretted shootings under similar circumstances before – but at the time it is likely that his concern was not with the ethics of encounter, but the necessity of escape. In other words, if Cook did instruct those in the boats to cease fire, he did so in order to have them concentrate on taking him and his party off. Given that a number of witnesses clearly 'imagined' such an instruction, it is likely that he uttered something to this effect; and he may well have done so, even though he did (as Phillips reports and Samwell denies) in fact order those marines who were on shore to fire. What was 'imagined' may thus have a basis in fact, but the action described had a practical rather than principled character; it was distorted in the image that emerged of Cook as a victim of his own humanity.

Yet if this is the overall tenor of Samwell's pamphlet, he does not over-emphasize it in the actual explanation of the circumstances. He acknow-ledges rather that the violence was not premeditated. 'This most melancholy accident, appears to have been altogether unexpected and unforeseen, as well on the part of the natives as ourselves.'[19] He places less weight on Cook's vulnerability at the moment he turned away from the Hawaiians to face the men in the boats and more on the failure – notorious among Cook enthusiasts – of Lieutenant Williamson to bring the launch he commanded to the shore at the crucial juncture. It is indeed a mystery as to why Williamson took his boat further offshore at this moment. His story was that he misunderstood Cook's signal. Samwell does not explicitly charge him with cowardice or incompetence, but anticipates many other writers in finding this withdrawal of additional support crucial and culpable. 'This circumstance appears to me, to have decided the fatal turn of the affair, and to have removed every chance which remained with Captain Cook, of escaping with his life', Samwell wrote. [20]

The *Narrative of the Death of Captain James Cook* draws closely upon a passage in Samwell's journal that is dated Sunday 14 February but seems too polished to have been written on the day itself. [21] The published text has been abbreviated at points but also elaborated upon; detail that Samwell might have considered superfluous has been removed; explanation that it did not occur to him to include in his journal is occasionally added; the text has generally been polished stylistically. For example, in the manuscript:

> [Cook] landed with the Marines at the Town on the most convenient Spot for drawing them up. The Indians immediately flocked round him as usual, without any hostile appearance, but not choosing to trust to this he was careful to have them kept at a proper distance from his men; he enquired for the two Boys the King's Sons, upon which two Messengers were directly sent for them, the 2 boys soon arrived and he asked them for their Father, they told him that he was asleep at a House in the Town a little distance off and he accompanied them thither with the Marines. [22]

In the published *Narrative*, this becomes:

> He landed, with the marines, at the upper end of the town of Kavaroah: the Indians immediately flocked round, as usual, and shewed him the customary marks of respect, by prostrating themselves before him. There were no signs of hostilities, or much alarm among them. Captain Cook, however, did not seem willing to trust to appearances; but was particularly attentive to the disposition of the marines, and to have them kept clear of the crowd. He first enquired for the king's sons, two youths who were much attached to him, and generally his companions on board. Messengers being sent for them, they soon came to him, and informing him that their father was asleep, at a house not far from them, he accompanied them thither, and took the marines along with them. [23]

This degree of revision is representative. There are a few more consequential changes. The manuscript sentence 'a Volley of Stones now came among our People on which the Marines gave a general fire' becomes the sentence quoted above; the Hawaiians 'poured a volley of stones among the marines, who, without waiting for orders, returned it with a general discharge'. But in general these alterations make explicit or lend force to a view of the incident that Samwell formed very soon after it occurred. His journal notes that after Cook gave up the idea of taking Kalaniopu'u off, he 'acted entirely on the defensive in order to secure a safe and orderly Embarkation for his small party into the boats'. This is fully consistent with, and indeed the theme of, the printed *Narrative*.

Samwell's pamphet included two further sections. The first briefly reviewed Cook's life and character. Although it includes minor errors of fact (such as the date of Cook's birth), the biographical section is generally accurate, and it is notable that Samwell apparently took the trouble to visit Cook's birthplace in order to obtain information. The account of the hero's character helped consolidate what had already become a conventional emphasis on Cook's benevolence and humanity.

The final section dealt with 'The introduction of the venereal disease into the Sandwich Islands'. Though this may appear to deal with an un-related issue of medical history, the morality of sexually transmitted disease in the Pacific had already been extensively debated. It is worth recalling that syphilis and gonorrhoea were widespread in the eighteenth century, associated with painful and repulsive symptoms such as facial corrosion, and were essentially incurable, though often treated with toxic mercury-based remedies. They were also, predictably enough, associated with moral degeneration. Although few would expect sailors to refrain from casual sexual encounters in ports, the project of exploration in the islands of the Pacific, which meant contacts with peoples long separated from their distant neighbours in Asia, raised the possibility, indeed the inevitability, that peoples among whom venereal diseases were unknown would be in-fected. The suffering that this would bring to individuals, and the longer-term harm to local populations, was well understood, and the communication of diseases therefore considered as appalling and reprehensible.

The issue was a peculiarly difficult one for those responsible for voyages of discovery, upon which a far higher degree of public interest focused than ever would on trading or normal naval operations. By the time of the 1769 visit in the *Endeavour*, it was clear that Tahitians were infected with a 'venereal Itch'. Debate has proceeded almost ever since about whether the British under Wallis or the French under Bougainville were responsible. Cook subsequently regretted the manifest damage to Maori, who were infected by his own crew. Men were examined by the surgeons, and those considered infected were not permitted on shore; in some places women were not allowed aboard the ships. Cook routinely complained that these restrictions were flouted. Even when they were not, they cannot have been fully effective. As he suspected, those who did not exhibit symptoms were sometimes able to infect others.

If Cook became somewhat alienated from his men during the course of the third voyage, his anger over their unrestrained sexual behaviour was one of the main causes of this disaffection, not least because Cook was tremendously conscious of both publicity and posterity. The issue became particularly pressing when places such as the Tongan islands and most especially the Hawaiian group were visited. Here, the people had not already been contacted by Wallis or by the French. If they suffered, it was Cook's responsibility. His men, he felt, betrayed him and the reputation of the voyage that, as far as it was in his power, he laboured to refine and enhance.

Samwell's excursus therefore supplements his vindication of Cook with a vindication of the voyage. He conceeds that both Cook and King believed that the inhabitants of the Hawaiian archipelago 'received that distemper from our people'. And indeed, it was widely noted in the voyage journals that on arrival off the coast of Molokai in late 1778, people displaying symptoms of 'the Clap' came off in canoes. They clearly associated the affliction with the British visit to Kauai at the beginning of that year, and hoped therefore that the British would carry medications that would relieve it. This – together with a wider pattern of evidence – is fairly conclusive. But Samwell insists that Cook's precautions were effective, and asserted that it was very improbable that the disease would in fact be carried as far as from Kauai to the eastern end of the archipelago, in as short a time as ten months. To these points it may be answered that there is explicit evidence in the journals that Cook's precautions at Kauai did not prevent sexual contacts; and secondly that there was regular inter-island contact within the Hawaiian group, and hence nothing inherently improbable about the transmission of these conditions over the period in question. Given Samwell's participation in the activities that Cook had censured, and that had such a disastrous impact on the health of Hawaiians, it is not surprising that he was prompted to advance contrived and un-convincing arguments that excused the expedition, and by implication himself, from actions regarded as horribly criminal by some people at the time, even by some of those who sailed with Cook, such as Forster and Anderson. David Samwell was for the most part an honest, perceptive and acute observer, but on this occasion these traits deserted him.

Note on the texts

A Narrative of the Death of Captain James Cook . . . is reproduced from the only London edition, printed by G. G. J. and J. Robinson in 1786. Samwell's spelling and punctuation have been retained. Within this text, Samwell's notes are designated by asterisks and appear at the foot of the page. The editors' notes are numbered and appear at the end of this text. The relationship of this text to the relevant passage in Samwell's journal is discussed in Nicholas Thomas's chapter, above. An intermediate version appears as an extended footnote to the Cook entry in Andrew Kippis, *Biographia Britannica: or, the lives of the most eminent persons who have flourished in Great-Britain and Ireland* (London, 1784; 2nd edn, 1789), vol. IV, pp. 230–34. This commences with the paragraph beginning 'On the sixth . . .' (that is, the second paragraph of the main text), and concludes with 'the trophies they make of his bones' at the end of that main section of the text; neither the sketch of Cook's life nor the essay on the introduction of venereal disease was published by Kippis. A manuscript that is not in Samwell's hand is held by the State Library of New South Wales (MS Q153); in this, the account of Cook's life precedes the narrative of the death. There are minor variations of wording rather than substantive differences between these texts. The scope for annotation of any material related to Cook's voyages is almost unlimited, and we have aimed to be highly selective here, pointing toward other major sources and accessible recent commentaries and controversies, while refraining from point-by-point comparisons between Samwell's account and those of other third-voyage participants, or full ethnographic and historical contextualization, which would generally entail repeating information that is readily accessible to interested readers in other works.

The correspondence

From the Samwell-Gregson correspondence in the Liverpool Record Office (LRO 920 GRE 2/17) we have printed all the letters from Samwell relating to his participation in Cook's third voyage, and excerpts from a few letters of more marginal relevance. The manuscripts are not in a perfect condition; the edges of some of the letters are ragged, and in other cases are torn where the seal has been broken. Where there are complete gaps, especially where there may be one or more whole words missing, they are indicated by three periods . . . Where a word is incomplete, it has been completed in parenthesis in cases where the missing letters necessary to complete that word are likely, sometimes because part of them can still be seen; a question mark is placed within the parenthesis where there is a considerable element of doubt. The capitalization does not follow Samwell's original, and has been retained only where it is felt appropriate.

The Poetry

There appear to be two extant copies of the poem on St David's Day, 1 March 1777, one in the National Library of Wales, Cwrt Mawr Manuscripts (MS35B) (NRA 29236 Davies), which is printed in William Llewelyn Davies's article on Samwell ('David Samwell (1751–1798)', 89–90), and reprinted and translated here, and the other in Cardiff Central Library, MS 3.116 (79), which is also available on microfilm in the National Library of Wales.

The 'Ode for the New Year, 1790' was printed as a broadsheet. It is extant in the British Library (Add. MS 1495, f.117), and is republished here for the first time. The end of the sheet reads 'Compos'd By Mr David Samwell Fetter Lane London'.

'Ode, Dec. 24, 1794', was published in the *Gentleman's Magazine*, February 1795. Anna Seward noted that the winter of 1794/5 had been 'relentless', but deemed the ode to have a 'happy, and I think Horatian spirit' (*Letters of Anna Seward*, IV, p. 40, to Samwell, 17 March 1795).

'The Padouca Hunt' was published posthumously in 1799 in *The Commercial and Agricultural Magazine* volume I. A facsimile was published in W. Llewelyn Davies's article on David Samwell, and he subsequently published an edited version with an introduction in *The National Library of Wales Journal*, II (1941–2).

'The Negro Boy' was printed as a broadsheet by J. Young of Bristol. It is undated and may have been printed after Samwell's death, as Young is known in Bristol only from the late 1790s until his death in 1806. However, in this case, it is likely to have printed elsewhere earlier, since it is favourably mentioned in Samwell's *Gentleman's Magazine* obituary (see Davies, 'David Samwell: A Further Note', 257–9, and the broadsheet in the National Library of Wales).

Within the poetry, the footnotes are Samwell's except where indicated as (Eds) or (Trans.).

Notes

[1] For general background see Beaglehole, *Journals*, II and III; Beaglehole, *Life*; E. H. McCormack, *Omai* (Auckland: Auckland University Press and Oxford University Press, 1977); Anne Salmond, *The Trial of the Cannibal Dog* (London: Penguin, 2003); and Nicholas Thomas, *Discoveries: The Voyages of Captain James Cook* (London: Penguin, 2003).

2   See Glyn Williams, *Voyages of Delusion: The Search for the Northwest Passage in the Age of Reason* (London: HarperCollins, 2002).

3   George Forster, *A Voyage Round the World*, ed. N. Thomas and O. Berghof (Honolulu: University of Hawai'i Press, 2000), pp. 7–8.

4   Samwell, 'Some Account of a Voyage to the South Seas', Appendix II to Beaglehole, *Journals*, p. 1009.

5   Samwell, 'Some Account of a Voyage', pp. 1041, 1039.

6   Samwell, 'Some Account of a Voyage', pp. 1021–2, cf. p. 1049.

7   See Elizabeth Bott, *Tongan Society at the Time of Captain Cook's Visits* (Wellington: Polynesian Society, 1982).

8   Some sense of the proliferation of later editions may be gained from M. K. Beddie, *Bibliography of Captain James Cook* (Sydney: [State] Library of New South Wales, 1970), which, though based on extensive research, is incomplete in its listing of nineteenth- and twentieth-century popular and derivative material.

9   Beaglehole, *Journals*, pp. 528–40 reproduces James King's and Charles Clerke's accounts of this period. Note 2 to p. 536 quotes a number of other journals on Cook's death itself.

10   James King and Charles Ryskamp (eds), *The Letters and Prose Writings of William Cowper* (Oxford, 1981), II, pp. 282–83.

11   Twain, quoted in Jonathan Lamb, Vanessa Smith and Nicholas Thomas (eds), *Exploration and Exchange* (Chicago: University of Chicago Press, 2000), pp. 281–4; J. F. G. Stokes, 'Origins of the Condemnation of Captain Cook in Hawaii', *Report of the Hawaiian Historical Society for 1930*.

12   See Bernard Smith, *European Vision and the South Pacific* (New Haven: Yale University Press, second edn, 1985), and Bernard Smith, *Imagining the Pacific* (New Haven: Yale University Press, 1992).

13   Marshall Sahlins, *Historical Metaphors and Mythical Realities: Structure in the Early History of the Sandwich Islands Kingdom* (Ann Arbor: University of Michigan Press, 1981); Marshall Sahlins, *Islands of History* (Chicago: University of Chicago Press, 1985); Gananath Obeyesekere, *The Apotheosis of Captain Cook* (Princeton: Princeton University Press, 1992); Marshall Sahlins, *How 'Natives' Think, about Captain Cook for example* (Chicago: University of Chicago Press, 1995). For a useful review of the controversy, see Rob Borofsky, 'Cook, Lono, Obeyesekere, Sahlins', *Current Anthropology*, 38 (1997), 255–82.

14   Beaglehole, *Journals*, pp. clii–clvii.

15   James Cook and James King, *A Voyage to the Pacific Ocean . . .* (London: Strahan and Cadell, 1784), III, pp. 45–6.

16   Cook and King, *A Voyage*, III, p. 49.

17   Obeyesekere, *Apotheosis*, pp. 104–5.

18   See p. 75 this volume.

19   See p. 78 this volume.

20   See p. 76 this volume.

21   Beaglehole, *Journals*, pp. 1194–201.

22   Beaglehole, *Journals*, p. 1195.

23   See p. 72 this volume.

Hawaiian drum (a high-pitched *puniu*), believed to have been in David Samwell's collection. Coconut shell, skin (shark?), wood, coconut fibre, 20.5cm x 12cm. Hunterian Museum and Art Gallery, University of Glasgow, E.367.

A

N A R R A T I V E

OF THE

D E A T H

OF

CAPTAIN JAMES COOK.

TO WHICH ARE ADDED SOME

P A R T I C U L A R S,

CONCERNING HIS

LIFE AND CHARACTER.

AND

O B S E R V A T I O N S

RESPECTING THE

I N T R O D U C T I O N

OF THE

V E N E R E A L   D I S E A S E

INTO THE

S A N D W I C H   I S L A N D S.

———

BY D A V I D S A M W E L L,

SURGEON OF THE DISCOVERY.

———

L O N D O N:

PRINTED FOR G. G. J. AND J. ROBINSON, PATER-NOSTER-ROW.
MDCCLXXXVI.

Title-page, *A Narrative of the Death of Captain Cook*, London: G. G. J. and J. Robinson, 1786. British Library, London, 814.l.2.

A Narrative of the Death of Captain James Cook

Preface

To those who have perused the account of the last voyage to the Pacific Ocean, [1] the following sheets may, at first sight, appear superfluous. The author, however, being of opinion, that the event of Captain Cook's death has not yet been so explicitly related as the importance of it required, trusts that this Narrative will not be found altogether a repetition of what is already known. At the same time, he wishes to add his humble testimony to the merit of the account given of this transaction by Captain King. Its brevity alone can afford an excuse for this publication, the object of which is to give a more particular relation of that unfortunate affair, which he finds is in general but imperfectly understood. He thinks himself warranted in saying this, from having frequently observed, that the public opinion seemed to attribute the loss of Captain Cook's life, in some measure, to rashness or too much confidence on his side; whereas nothing can be more ill-founded or unjust. It is, therefore, a duty which his friends owe to his character, to have the whole affair candidly and fully related, whatever facts it may involve, that may appear of a disagreeable nature to individuals. The author is confident, that if Captain King could have foreseen, that any wrong opinion respecting Captain Cook, would have been the consequence of omitting some circumstances relative to his death; the good-natured motive that induced him to be silent, would not have stood a moment in competition with the superior call of justice to the memory of his friend. This publication, he is satisfied, would not have been disapproved of by Captain King, for whose memory he has the highest esteem, and to whose friendship he is under many obligations. [2] He is sanguine enough to believe, that it will serve to remove a supposition in this single instance, injurious to the memory of Captain Cook, who was no less distinguished for his caution and prudence, than for his eminent abilities and undaunted resolution.

The late appearance of this Narrative has been owing to the peculiar situation of the writer, whose domestic residence is at a great distance from the metropolis, and whose duty frequently calls him from home for several months together. He has the pleasure of adding, that, in publishing the following account of Captain Cook's death, he acts in concurrence with the opinion of some very respectable persons. [3]

John Webber, 'Kalaniopuu, King of Owyhee, Bringing Presents to Captain Cook', c.1781–83, pen, ink-wash and watercolour, 22cm x 37.8cm. Dixson Library, State Library of New South Wales, Sydney, PXX2. fo.35.

A Narrative of the Death of Captain Cook

In the month of January, 1779, the Resolution and Discovery lay about a fortnight at anchor in the bay of Kerag,e,goo,ah*, in the Island of Ou,why,ee.[4] During that time, the ships were most plentifully supplied with provisions by the natives, with whom we lived on the most friendly terms. We were universally treated by them with kind attention and hospitality; but the respect they paid to Captain Cook, was little short of adoration. It was, therefore, with sentiments of the most perfect good-will towards the inhabitants, that we left the harbour, on the fourth of February. It was Captain Cook's intention to visit the other islands to leeward, and we stood to the westward, towards Mowee, attended by several canoes full of people, who were willing to accompany us as far as they could, before they bad us a final adieu.

On the sixth, we were overtaken by a gale of wind; and the next night, the Resolution had the misfortune of springing the head of her foremast, in such a dangerous manner, that Captain Cook was obliged to return to Keragegooah, in order to have it repaired; for we could find no other convenient harbour on the island. The same gale had occasioned much distress among some canoes, that had paid us a visit from the shore. One of them, with two men and a child on board, was picked up by the Resolution, and rescued from destruction: the men, having toiled hard all night, in attempting

---

*   I take it for granted, that most of those into whose hands these pages may fall, have perused Captain Cook's last Voyage, and therefore, I have all along mentioned the names of the principal actors in this account, as people with whom they are already acquainted. But as I differ so much in the orthography of the language of the Sandwich Islands from that used in the printed Voyage, it becomes necessary for me to explain the names I use in this narrative, by those already known. It may appear strange, how we should differ so much; but so it is:–which is the most accurate, some future visiter may determine.

Karakakooa	I call	Ke,rag,e,goo,ah,
Terreeoboo	–	Kariopoo,
Kowrowa		Kavaroah,
Kaneecabareea		Kaneekapo,herei,
Maiha maiha		Ka,mea,mea.

to reach the land, were so much exhausted, that they could hardly mount the ship's side. When they got upon the quarter-deck, they burst into tears, and seemed much affected with the dangerous situation from which they had escaped; but the little child appeared lively and cheerful. One of the Resolution's boats was also so fortunate as to save a man and two women, whose canoe had been upset by the violence of the waves. They were brought on board, and, with the others, partook of the kindness and humanity of Captain Cook.

On the morning of Wednesday, the tenth, we were within a few miles of the harbour; and were soon joined by several canoes, in which appeared many of our old acquaintance, who seemed to have come to welcome us back. [5] Among them was Coo,aha, a priest: he had brought a small pig, and some cocoa nuts in his hand, which, after having chaunted a few sentences, he presented to Captain Clerke. He then left us, and hastened on board the Resolution, to perform the same friendly ceremony before Captain Cook. Having but light winds all that day, we could not gain the harbour. In the afternoon, a chief of the first rank, and nearly related to Kariopoo,[6] paid us a visit on board the Discovery. His name was Ka,mea,mea:[7] he was dressed in a very rich feathered cloke, which he seemed to have brought for sale, but would part with it for nothing except iron daggers. [8] These, the chiefs, some time before our departure, had preferred to every other article; for having received a plentiful supply of hatchets and other tools, they began to collect a store of warlike instruments. Kameamea procured nine daggers for his cloke, and being pleased with his reception, he and his attendants slept on board that night.

In the morning of the eleventh of February, the ships anchored again in Keragegooah bay, and preparation was immediately made for landing the Resolution's foremast. [9] We were visited but by few of the Indians, because there were but few in the bay. On our departure, those belonging to other parts, had repaired to their several habitations, and were again to collect from various quarters, before we could expect to be surrounded by such multitudes as we had once seen in that harbour. In the afternoon, I walked about a mile into the country, to visit an Indian friend, who had, a few days before, come near twenty miles, in a small canoe, to see me, while the ship lay becalmed. As the canoe had not left us long before a gale of wind came on, I was alarmed for the consequence: however, I had the pleasure to find that my friend had escaped unhurt, though not without some difficulties. I take notice of this short excursion, merely because it afforded me an opportunity of observing, that there appeared no change in the disposition or behaviour of the inhabitants. I saw nothing that could induce me to think, that they were displeased with our return or jealous of the intention of our second visit. On the contrary, that abundant good nature which had always characterised them, seemed still to glow in every bosom, and to animate every countenance.

The next day, February the twelfth, the ships were put under a taboo, by the chiefs, a solemnity, it seems, that was requisite to be observed before Kariopoo, the king, paid his first visit to Captain Cook, after his return. He waited upon him the same day, on board the Resolution, attended by a large train, some of which bore the presents designed for Captain Cook, who received him in his usual friendly manner, and gave him several articles in return. This amicable ceremony being settled, the taboo was dissolved, matters went on in the usual train, and the next day, February the thirteenth, we were visited by the natives in great numbers; the Resolution's mast was landed, and the astronomical observatories erected on their former situation. I landed, with another gentleman, at the town of Kavaroah, [10] where we found a great number of canoes, just arrived from different parts of the island, and the Indians busy in constructing temporary huts on the beach, for their residence during the stay of the ships. On our return on board the Discovery, we learned, that an Indian had been detected in stealing the armourer's tongs from the forge, for which he received a pretty severe flogging, and was sent out of the ship. Notwithstanding the example made of this man, in the afternoon another had the audacity to snatch the tongs and a chizel from the same place, with which he jumped overboard, and swam for the shore. The master and a midshipman were instantly dispatched after him, in the small cutter. The Indian seeing himself pursued, made for a canoe; his countrymen took him on board, and paddled as swift as they could towards the shore; we fired several muskets at them, but to no effect, for they soon got out of the reach of our shot. Pareah, one of the chiefs, who was at that time on board the Discovery, understanding what had happened, immediately went ashore, promising to bring back the stolen goods. Our boat was so far distanced, in chasing the canoe which had taken the thief on board, that he had time to make his escape into the country. Captain Cook, who was then on shore, endeavoured to intercept his landing; but, it seems, that he was led out of the way by some of the natives, who had officiously intruded themselves as guides. As the master was approaching near the landing-place, he was met by some of the Indians in a canoe: they had brought back the tongs and chizel together with another article, that we had not missed, which happened to be the lid of the water-cask. Having recovered these things, he was returning on board when he was met by the Resolution's pinnace, with five men in her, who, without any orders, had come from the observatories to his assistance. Being thus unexpectedly reinforced, he thought himself strong enough to insist upon having the thief, or the canoe which took him in, delivered up as reprizals. With that view he turned back; and having found the canoe on the beach, he was preparing to launch it into the water, when Pareah made his appearance and insisted upon his not taking it away, as it was his property. The officer not regarding him, the chief seized upon him, pinioned his arms behind, and held him by the hair of his head; on which, one of the sailors struck him with an oar: Pareah instantly quitted the officer, snatched the oar out of the man's hand, and snapped it in two across his knee. At length, the multitude began to attack our people with stones. They made some resistance, but were soon overpowered, and obliged to swim for safety to the small cutter, which lay farther out than the pinnace. The officers, not being expert swimmers, retreated to a small rock in the water, where they were closely pursued by the Indians. One man darted a broken oar at the master; but his foot slipping at the time, he missed him, which fortunately saved that officer's life. At last, Pareah interfered, and put an end to their violence. The Gentlemen, knowing that his presence was their only defence against the fury of the natives, entreated him to stay with them, till they could get off in the boats; but that he refused, and left them. The master went to seek assistance from the party at the observatories; but the midshipman chose to remain in the pinnace. He was very rudely treated by the mob, who plundered the boat of every thing that was loose on board, and then began to knock her to pieces, for the sake of the iron-work; but Pareah fortunately returned in time to prevent her destruction. He had met the other gentleman on his way to the observatories, and suspecting his errand, had forced him to return. He dispersed the crowd again, and desired the gentlemen to return on board: they represented, that all the oars had been taken out of the boat; on which he brought some of them back, and the gentlemen were glad to get off, without farther molestation. They had not proceeded far, before they were overtaken by Pareah in a canoe: he delivered the midshipman's cap which had been taken from him in the scuffle, joined noses with them, in token of reconciliation, and was anxious to know, if Captain Cook would kill him for what had happened. They assured him of the contrary, and made signs of friendship to him in return. He then left them, and paddled over to the town of Kavaroah, and that was the last time we ever saw him. Captain Cook returned on board soon after, much displeased with the whole of this disagreeable business; and the same night, sent a lieutenant on board the Discovery, to learn the particulars of it, as it had originated in that ship. [11]

It was remarkable, that in the midst of the hurry and confusion attending this affair, Kanynah (a chief who had always been on terms particularly friendly with us) came from the spot where it happened, with a hog to sell on board the Discovery: it was of an extraordinary large size, and he demanded for it a pahowa, or dagger, of an unusual length. He pointed to us, that it must be as long as his arm. Captain Clerke not having one of that length, told him, he would get one made for him by the morning; with which being satisfied, he left the hog, and went ashore without making any stay with us. It will not be altogether foreign to the subject, to mention a circumstance, that happened to-day on board the Resolution. An Indian chief asked Captain Cook at his table, if he was a *Tata Toa*; which means a fighting man, [12] or a soldier. Being answered in the affirmative, he desired to see his wounds: Captain Cook held out his right-hand, which had a scar upon it, dividing the thumb from the finger, the whole length of the metacarpal bones. [13] The Indian, being thus convinced of his being a Toa, put the same question to another gentleman present, but he happened to have none of those distinguishing marks: the chief then said, that he himself was a Toa, and shewed the scars of some wounds he had received in battle. Those who were on duty at the observatories, were disturbed during the night, with shrill and melancholy sounds, issuing from the adjacent villages, which they took to be the lamentations of the women. Perhaps the quarrel between us, might have filled their minds with apprehensions for the safety of their husbands: but, be that as it may, their mournful cries struck the sentinels with unusual awe and terror.

To widen the breach between us, some of the Indians, in the night, took away the Discovery's large cutter, which lay swamped at the buoy of one of her anchors: [14] they had carried her off so quietly, that we did not miss her till the morning, Sunday, February the fourteenth. Captain Clerke lost no time in waiting upon Captain Cook, to acquaint him with the accident: he returned on board, with orders for the launch and small cutter to go, under the command of the second lieutenant, and lie off the east point of the bay, in order to intercept all canoes that might attempt to get out; and, if he found it necessary, to fire upon them. At the same time, the third lieutenant of the Resolution, with the launch and small cutter, was sent on the same service, to the opposite point of the bay; and the master was dispatched in the large cutter, in pursuit of a double canoe, already under sail, making the best of her way out of the harbour. He soon came up with her, and by firing a few muskets, drove her on shore, and the Indians left her: this happened to be the canoe of Omea, a man who bore the title of Orono. He was on board himself, and it would have been fortunate, if our people had secured him, for his person was held as sacred as that of the king. During this time, Captain Cook was preparing to go ashore himself, at the town of Kavaroah, in order to secure the person of Kariopoo, before he should have time to withdraw himself to another part of the island, out of our reach. This appeared the most effectual step that could be taken on the present occasion, for the recovery of the boat. It was the measure he had invariably pursued, in similar cases, at other islands in these seas, and it had always been attended with the desired success: in fact, it would be difficult to point out any other mode of proceeding on these emergencies, likely to attain the object in view. [15] We had reason to suppose, that the king and his attendants had fled when the alarm was first given: in that case, it was Captain Cook's intention to secure the large canoes which were hauled up on the beach. He left the ship about seven o'clock, attended by the lieutenant of marines, a serjeant, corporal, and seven private men: the pinnace's crew were also armed, and under the command of Mr Roberts. As they rowed towards the shore, Captain Cook ordered the launch to leave her station at the west point of the bay, in order to assist his own boat. This is a circumstance worthy of notice; for it clearly shews, that he was not unapprehensive of meeting with resistance from the natives, or unmindful of the necessary preparation for the safety of himself and his people. I will venture to say, that from the appearance of things just at that time, there was not one, beside himself, who judged that such precaution was absolutely requisite: so little did his conduct on the occasion, bear the marks of rashness, or a precipitate self-confidence! He landed, with the marines, at the upper end of the town of Kavaroah: the Indians immediately flocked round, as usual, and shewed him the customary marks of respect, by prostrating themselves before him. There were no signs of hostilities, or much alarm among them. Captain Cook, however, did not seem willing to trust to appearances; but was particularly attentive to the disposition of the marines, and to have them kept clear of the crowd. He first enquired for the king's sons, two youths who were much attached to him, and generally his companions on board. Messengers being sent for them, they soon came to him, and informing him that their father was asleep, at a house not far from them, he accompanied them thither, and took the marines along with them. As he passed along, the natives every where prostrated themselves before him, and seemed to have lost no part of that respect they had always shewn to his person. He was joined by several chiefs, among whom was Kanynah, and his brother Koohowrooah. They kept the crowd in order, according to their usual custom; and being ignorant of his intention in coming on shore, frequently asked him, if he wanted any hogs, or other provisions: he told them that he did not, and that his business was to see the king. When he arrived at the house, he ordered some of the Indians to go in, and inform Kariopoo, that he waited without to speak with him. They came out two or three times, and instead of returning any answer from the king, presented some pieces of red cloth to him, which made Captain Cook suspect that he was not in the house; he therefore desired the lieutenant of marines to go in. The lieutenant found the old man just awaked from sleep, and seemingly

John Webber, 'A Chief of the Sandwich Islands Leading His Party to Battle', 1787, oil on canvas, 144.7cm x 93.5cm. National Library of Australia, Canberra, PIC T265 NK1.

alarmed at the message; but he came out without hesitation. Captain Cook took him by the hand, and in a friendly manner, asked him to go on board, to which he very readily consented. Thus far matters appeared in a favourable train, and the natives did not seem much alarmed or apprehensive of hostility on our side; at which Captain Cook expressed himself a little surprised, saying, that as the inhabitants of that town appeared innocent of stealing the cutter, he should not molest them, but that he must get the king on board. Kariopoo sat down before his door, and was surrounded by a great crowd: Kanynah and his brother were both very active in keeping order among them. In a little time, however, the Indians were observed arming themselves with long spears, clubs, and daggers, and putting on thick mats, which they use as armour. This hostile appearance increased, and became more alarming, on the arrival of two men in a canoe from the opposite side of the bay, with the news of a chief, called Kareemoo, having been killed by one of the Discovery's boats, in their passage across: they had also delivered this account to each of the ships. Upon that information, the women, who were sitting upon the beach at their breakfasts, and conversing familiarly with our people in the boats, retired, and a confused murmur spread through the crowd. An old priest came to Captain Cook, with a cocoa nut in his hand, which he held out to him as a present, at the same time singing very loud. He was often desired to be silent, but in vain: he continued importunate and troublesome, and there was no such thing as getting rid of him or his noise: it seemed, as if he meant to divert their attention from his countrymen, who were growing more tumultuous, and arming themselves in every quarter. Captain Cook, being at the same time surrounded by a great crowd, thought his situation rather hazardous: he therefore ordered the lieutenant of marines to march his small party to the water-side, where the boats lay within a few yards of the shore: the Indians readily made a lane for them to pass, and did not offer to interrupt them. The distance they had to go might be about fifty or sixty yards; Captain Cook followed, having hold of Kariopoo's hand, who accompanied him very willingly: he was attended by his wife, two sons, and several chiefs. The troublesome old priest followed, making the same savage noise. Keowa, the younger son, went directly into the pinnace, expecting his father to follow; but just as he arrived at the water-side, his wife threw her arms about his neck, and, with the assistance of two chiefs forced him to sit down by the side of a double canoe. Captain Cook expostulated with them, but to no purpose: they would not suffer the king to proceed, telling him, that he would be put to death if he went on board the ship. Kariopoo, whose conduct seemed entirely resigned to the will of others, hung down his head, and appeared much distressed.

While the king was in this situation, a chief, well known to us, of the name of Coho, was observed lurking near, with an iron dagger, partly concealed under his cloke, seemingly, with the intention of stabbing Captain Cook, or the lieutenant of marines. The latter proposed to fire at him, but Captain Cook would not permit it. Coho closing upon them, obliged the officer to strike him with his piece, which made him retire. Another Indian laid hold of the serjeant's musket, and endeavoured to wrench it from him, but was prevented by the lieutenant's making a blow at him. Captain Cook, seeing the tumult increase, and the Indians growing more daring and resolute, observed, that if he were to take the king off by force, he could not do it without sacrificing the lives of many of his people. He then paused a little, and was on the point of giving his orders to reimbark, when a man threw a stone at him; which he returned with a discharge of small shot, (with which one barrel of his double piece was loaded). The man, having a thick mat before him, received little or no hurt: he brandished his spear, and threatened to dart it at Captain Cook, who being still unwilling to take away his life, instead of firing with ball, knocked him down with his musket. He expostulated strongly with the most forward of the crowd, upon their turbulent behaviour. He had given up all thoughts of getting the king on board, as it appeared impracticable; and his care was then only to act on the defensive, and to secure a safe embarkation for his small party, which was closely pressed by a body of several thousand people. Keowa, the king's son, who was in the pinnace, being alarmed on hearing the first firing, was, at his own entreaty, put on shore again; for even at that time, Mr Roberts, who commanded her, did not apprehend that Captain Cook's person was in any danger: otherwise he would have detained the prince, which, no doubt, would have been a great check on the Indians. One man was observed, behind a double canoe, in the action of darting his spear at Captain Cook, who was forced to fire at him in his own defence, but happened to kill another close to him, equally forward in the tumult: the serjeant observing that he had missed the man he aimed at, received orders to fire at him, which he did, and killed him. By this time, the impetuosity of the Indians was somewhat repressed; they fell back in a body, and seemed staggered: but being pushed on by those behind, they returned to the charge, and poured a volley of stones among the marines, who, without waiting for orders, returned it with a general discharge of musketry, which was instantly followed by a fire from the boats. At this Captain Cook was heard to express his astonishment: he waved his hand to the boats, called to them to cease firing, and to come nearer in to receive the marines. Mr Roberts immediately brought the pinnace as close to the shore as he could, without grounding, notwithstanding the showers of stones that fell among the people: but Mr John

Williamson, the lieutenant, who commanded in the launch, instead of pulling in to the assistance of Captain Cook, withdrew his boat further off, at the moment that every thing seems to have depended upon the timely exertions of those in the boats. By his own account, he mistook the signal: but be that as it may, this circumstance appears to me, to have decided the fatal turn of the affair, and to have removed every chance which remained with Captain Cook, of escaping with his life. The business of saving the marines out of the water, in consequence of that, fell altogether upon the pinnace; which thereby became so much crowded, that the crew were, in a great measure, prevented from using their fire-arms, or giving what assistance they otherwise might have done, to Captain Cook; so that he seems, at the most critical point of time, to have wanted the assistance of both boats, owing to the removal of the launch. For notwithstanding that they kept up a fire on the crowd from the situation to which they removed in that boat, the fatal confusion which ensued on her being withdrawn, to say the least of it, must have prevented the full effect, that the prompt co-operation of the two boats, according to Captain Cook's orders, must have had, towards the preservation of himself and his people. At that time, it was to the boats alone, that Captain Cook had to look for his safety; for when the marines had fired, the Indians rushed among them, and forced them into the water, where four of them were killed: their lieutenant was wounded, but fortunately escaped, and was taken up by the pinnace. Captain Cook was then the only one remaining on the rock: he was observed making for the pinnace, holding his left hand against the back of his head, to guard it from the stones, and carrying his musket under the other arm. An Indian was seen following him, but with caution and timidity; for he stopped once or twice, as if undetermined to proceed. At last he advanced upon him unawares, and with a large club*, or common stake, gave him a blow on the back of the head, and then precipitately retreated. The stroke seemed to have stunned Captain Cook: he staggered a few paces, then fell on his hand and one knee, and dropped his musket. As he was rising, and before he could recover his feet, another Indian stabbed him in the back of the neck with an iron dagger. He then fell into a bit of water about knee deep, where others crowded upon him, and endeavoured

---

*   I have heard one of the gentlemen who were present say, that the first injury he received was from a dagger, as it is represented in the Voyage; but, from the account of many others, who were also eye-witnesses, I am confident, in saying, that he was first struck with a club. I was afterwards confirmed in this, by Kaireekea, the priest, who particularly mentioned the name of the man who gave him the blow, as well as that of the chief who afterwards struck him with the dagger. This is a point not worth disputing about: I mention it, as being solicitous to be accurate in this account, even in circumstances, of themselves, not very material.

to keep him under: but struggling very strongly with them, he got his head up, and casting his look towards the pinnace, seemed to solicit assistance. Though the boat was not above five or six yards distant from him, yet from the crowded and confused state of the crew, it seems, it was not in their power to save him. The Indians got him under again, but in deeper water: he was, however, able to get his head up once more, and being almost spent in the struggle, he naturally turned to the rock, and was endeavouring to support himself by it, when a savage gave him a blow with a club, and he was seen alive no more. They hauled him up lifeless on the rocks, where they seemed to take a savage pleasure in using every barbarity to his dead body, snatching the daggers out of each other's hands, to have the horrid satisfaction of piercing the fallen victim of their barbarous rage. [16]

I need make no reflection on the great loss we suffered on this occasion, or attempt to describe what we felt. It is enough to say, that no man was ever more beloved or admired: and it is truly painful to reflect, that he seems to have fallen a sacrifice merely for want of being properly supported; a fate, singularly to be lamented, as having fallen to his lot, who had ever been conspicuous for his care of those under his command, and who seemed, to the last, to pay as much attention to their preservation, as to that of his own life.

If any thing could have added to the shame and indignation universally felt on the occasion, it was to find, that his remains had been deserted, and left exposed on the beach, although they might have been brought off. It appears, from the information of four or five midshipmen, who arrived on the spot at the conclusion of the fatal business, that the beach was then almost entirely deserted by the Indians, who at length had given way to the fire of the boats, and dispersed through the town: so that there seemed no great obstacle to prevent the recovery of Captain Cook's body; but the lieutenant returned on board without making the attempt. It is unnecessary to dwell longer on this painful subject, and to relate the complaints and censures that fell on the conduct of the lieutenant. It will be sufficient to observe, that they were so loud, as to oblige Captain Clerke publickly to notice them, and to take the depositions of his accusers down in writing. The Captain's bad state of health and approaching dissolution, it is supposed, induced him to destroy these papers a short time before his death.

It is a painful task, to be obliged to notice circumstances, which seem to reflect upon the character of any man. A strict regard to truth, however, compelled me to the insertion of these facts, which I have offered merely as facts, without presuming to connect with them any comment of my own: esteeming it the part of a faithful historian, 'to extenuate nothing, nor set down ought in malice'.

The fatal accident happened at eight o'clock in the morning, about an hour after Captain Cook landed. It did not seem, that the king, or his sons, were witnesses to it; but it is supposed that they withdrew in the midst of the tumult. The principal actors were the other chiefs, many of them the king's relations and attendants: the man who stabbed him with the dagger was called Nooah. I happened to be the only one who recollected his person, from having on a former occasion mentioned his name in the journal I kept. I was induced to take particular notice of him, more from his personal appearance than any other consideration, though he was of high rank, and a near relation of the king: he was stout and tall, with a fierce look and demeanour, and one who united in his figure the two qualities of strength and agility, in a greater degree, than ever I remembered to have seen before in any other man. His age might be about thirty, and by the white scurf on his skin, and his sore eyes, he appeared to be a hard drinker of Kava. He was a constant companion of the king, with whom I first saw him, when he paid a visit to Captain Clerke. The chief who first struck Captain Cook with the club, was called Karimano,craha, but I did not know him by his name. These circumstances I learnt of honest Kaireekea, the priest; who added, that they were both held in great esteem on account of that action: neither of them came near us afterwards. When the boats left the shore, the Indians carried away the dead body of Captain Cook and those of the marines, to the rising ground, at the back of the town, where we could plainly see them with our glasses from the ships.

This most melancholy accident, appears to have been altogether unexpected and unforeseen, as well on the part of the natives as ourselves. I never saw sufficient reason to induce me to believe, that there was any thing of design, or a pre-concerted plan on their side, or that they purposely sought to quarrel with us: thieving, which gave rise to the whole, they were equally guilty of, in our first and second visits. It was the cause of every misunderstanding that happened between us: their petty thefts were generally overlooked, but sometimes slightly punished: the boat, which they at last ventured to take away, was an object of no small magnitude to people in our situation, who could not possibly replace her, and therefore not slightly to be given up. We had no other chance of recovering her, but by getting the person of the king into our possession: on our attempting to do that, the natives became alarmed for his safety, and naturally opposed those whom they deemed his enemies. In the sudden conflict that ensued, we had the unspeakable misfortune of losing our excellent Commander, in the manner already related. It is in this light the affair has always appeared to me, as entirely accidental, and not in the least owing to any previous offence received, or jealousy of our second visit entertained by the natives.

Pareah seems to have been the principal instrument in bringing about this fatal disaster. We learnt afterwards, that it was he who had employed some people to steal the boat: the king did not seem to be privy to it, or even apprized of what had happened, till Captain Cook landed.

It was generally remarked, that at first, the Indians shewed great resolution in facing our fire-arms; but it was entirely owing to ignorance of their effect. They thought that their thick mats would defend them from a ball, as well as from a stone; but being soon convinced of their error, yet still at a loss to account how such execution was done among them, they had recourse to a stratagem, which, though it answered no other purpose, served to shew their ingenuity and quickness of invention. Observing the flashes of the muskets, they naturally concluded, that water would counter-act their effect, and therefore, very sagaciously, dipped their mats, or armour in the sea, just as they came on to face our people: but finding this last resource to fail them, they soon dispersed, and left the beach entirely clear. It was an object they never neglected, even at the greatest hazard, to carry off their slain; a custom, probably, owing to the barbarity with which they treat the dead body of an enemy, and the trophies they make of his bones.*

---

*   A remarkable instance of this I met with at Atowai. Tamataherei, the queen of that island, paid us a visit one day on board the Discovery, accompanied by her husband Taeòh, and one of her daughters by her former husband Oteeha. The young princess, whose name was Ore,reemo,horanee, carried in her hand a very elegant flyflap, of a curious construction: the upper part of it was variegated with alternate rings of tortoise-shell and human bone, and the handle, which was well polished, consisted of the greater part of the os humeri of a chief, called Mahowra. He had belonged to the neighbouring island of Oahoo, and, in a hostile descent he made upon this coast, had been killed by Oteeha, who was then sovereign of Atowai. And thus we found Orereemohoranee carrying his bones about, as trophies of her father's victory. The queen set a great value upon in, and was not willing to part with it for any of our iron ware; but happening to cast her eyes on a wash-hand bason of mine, it struck her fancy, and she offered to exchange; I accepted of her proposal, and the bones of the unfortunate Mahowra came at last into my possession.

Some Particulars, Concerning the Life and Character of Captain Cook

CAPTAIN COOK was born at Marton, in Cleaveland, in the county of York, a small village, distant five miles south-east from Stockton. His name is found in the parish register in the year 1729 (so that Captain King was mistaken, in placing the time of his birth in the year 1727). [17] The cottage in which his father formerly lived, is now decayed, but the spot where it stood is still shewn to strangers. A gentleman is now living in that neighbourhood, with whom the old man formerly worked as a common day-labourer in the fields. However, though placed in this humble station, he gave his son a common school education, and at an early age, placed him apprentice with one Mr Saunderson, a shopkeeper at Staith, (always pronounced Steers) a small fishing-town on the Yorkshire coast, about nine miles to the northward of Whitby. The business is now carried on by the son of Mr Saunderson, in the same shop, which I had the curiosity to visit about a year and half ago. In that situation young Cook did not continue long, before he quitted it in disgust, and, as often happens in the like cases, betook himself to the sea. Whitby being a neighbouring sea-port, readily offered him an opportunity to pursue his inclination; and there we find he bound himself apprentice, for nine years, in the coal trade, to one Mr John Walker now living in South Whitby. [18] In his employ, he afterwards became mate of a ship; in which station having continued some time, he had the offer of being master, which he refused, as it seems he had at that time turned his thoughts towards the navy. Accordingly, at the breaking out of the war in 1755, he entered on board the Eagle, of sixty-four guns, and in a short time after, Sir Hugh Palliser was appointed to the command of that ship, a circumstance that must not be passed unnoticed, as it proved the foundation of the future fame and fortune of Captain Cook. His uncommon merit did not long escape the observation of that discerning officer, who promoted him to the quarter-deck, and ever after patronized him with such zeal and attention, as must reflect the highest honour upon his character. To Sir Hugh Palliser is the world indebted, for having first noticed in an obscure situation, and afterwards brought forward in life, the greatest nautical genius that ever any age or country has produced. In the year 1758, we find him master of the Northumberland, then in America, under the command of Lord Colville. It was there, he has been heard to say, that during a hard winter he first read Euclid, and applied himself to the study of astronomy and the mathematics, in which he made no inconsiderable progress, assisted only by his own ingenuity and industry. At the time he thus found means to cultivate and improve his mind, and to supply the deficiency of an early education, he was constantly engaged in the most busy and active scenes of the war in America. At the siege of Quebec, Sir Hugh Palliser made him known to Sir Charles Saunders, who committed to his charge the conducting of the boats to the attack of mount Morenci, and the embarkation that scaled the heights of Abraham. He was also employed to examine the passage of the river St. Laurence, and to lay buoys for the direction of the men of war. In short, in whatever related to the reduction of that place in the naval department, he had a principal share, and conducted himself so well throughout the whole, as to recommend himself to the commander in chief. At the conclusion of the war, Sir Hugh Palliser having the command on the Newfoundland station, he appointed him to survey that Island and the coast of Labradore, and gave him the Grenville brig for that purpose. How well he performed that service, the charts he has published afford a sufficient testimony. In that employment he continued till the year 1767, when the well known voyage to the South Sea, for observing the transit of Venus, and making discoveries in that vast ocean was planned. Lord Hawke, who then presided at the Admiralty, was strongly solicited to give the command of that expedition to Mr Alexander Dalrymple; but through the interest of his friend Sir Hugh Palliser, Captain Cook obtained the appointment, together with the rank of lieutenant. It was stipulated, that on his return, he should, if he chose it, again hold the place of surveyor of Newfoundland, and that his family should be provided for, in case of any accident to himself.

He sailed from England in the Endeavour, in the year 1768, accompanied by Mr Banks and Dr. Solander, and returned in 1771; after having circumnavigated the globe, made several important discoveries in the South Sea, and explored the islands of New Zealand, and great part of the coast of New Holland. The skill and ability with which he conducted that expedition, ranked his name high as a navigator, and could not fail of recommending him to that great patron of naval merit, the Earl of Sandwich, who then presided at the board of Admiralty. He was promoted to the rank of master and commander, and a short time afterwards, appointed to conduct another expedition to the Pacific Ocean, in search of the supposed southern continent. In this second voyage he circumnavigated the globe, determined the non-existence of a southern continent, and added many valuable discoveries to those he had before made in the South Sea. His own account of it is before the public, and he is no less admired for the accuracy and extensive knowledge which he has displayed in that work, than for his skill and intrepidity in conducting the expedition. On his return, he was promoted to the rank of post-captain, and appointed one of the captains of Greenwich hospital. In that Retirement he did not continue long: for an active life best suiting his disposition, he offered his services to conduct a third expedition to the South Sea, which was then in agitation, in order to explore a northern passage from Europe to Asia: in this he unfortunately lost his life, but not till he had fully accomplished the object of the voyage.

The character of Captain Cook will be best exemplified by the services he has performed, which are universally known, and have ranked his name above that of any navigator of ancient or of modern times. Nature had endowed him with a mind vigorous and comprehensive, which in his riper years he had cultivated with care and industry. His general knowledge was extensive and various: in that of his own profession he was unequalled. With a clear judgement, strong masculine sense, and the most determined resolution; with a genius peculiarly turned for enterprize, he pursued his object with unshaken perseverance:—vigilant and active in an eminent degree:—cool and intrepid among dangers; patient and firm under difficulties and distress; fertile in expedients; great and original in all his designs; active and resolved in carrying them into execution. These qualities rendered him the animating spirit of the expedition: in every situation, he stood unrivalled and alone; on him all eyes were turned; he was our leading-star, which at its setting, left us involved in darkness and despair.

His constitution was strong, his mode of living temperate: why Captain King should not suppose temperance as great a virtue in him as any other man, I am unable to guess. He had no repugnance to good living; he always kept a good table, though he could bear the reverse without murmuring. He was a modest man, and rather bashful; of an agreeable lively conversation sensible and intelligent. In his temper he was somewhat hasty, but of a disposition the most friendly, benevolent, and humane. His person was above six feet high, and though a goodlooking man, he was plain both in address and appearance. His head was small, his hair, which was a dark brown, he wore tied behind. His face was full of expression, his nose exceedingly well-shaped, his eyes, which were small and of a brown cast, were quick and piercing: his eyebrows prominent, which gave his countenance altogether an air of austerity.

He was beloved by his people, who looked up to him as to a father, and obeyed his commands with alacrity. The confidence we placed in him was unremitting; our admiration of his great talents unbounded; our esteem for his good qualities affectionate and sincere.

In exploring unknown countries, the dangers he had to encounter were various and uncommon. On such occasions, he always displayed great presence of mind, and a steady perseverance in pursuit of his object. The acquisition he has made to our knowledge of the globe is immense, besides improving the art of navigation, and enriching the science of natural philosophy.

He was remarkably distinguished for the activity of his mind: it was that which enabled him to pay an unwearied attention to every object of the service. The strict oeconomy he observed in the expenditure of the ship's stores, and the unremitting care he employed for the preservation of the health of his people, were the causes that enabled him to prosecute discoveries in remote parts of the globe, for such a length of time as had been deemed impracticable by former navigators. The method he discovered for preserving the health of seamen in long voyages, will transmit his name to posterity as the friend and benefactor of mankind: the success which attended it, afforded this truly great man more satisfaction, than the distinguished fame that attended his discoveries.

England has been unanimous in her tribute of applause to his virtues, and all Europe has borne testimony to his merit. There is hardly a corner of the earth, however remote and savage, that will not long remember his benevolence and humanity. The grateful Indian, in time to come, pointing to the herds grazing his fertile plains, will relate to his children how the first stock of them was introduced into the country; and the name of Cook will be remembered among those benign spirits, whom they worship as the source of every good, and the fountain of every blessing. [19]

It may not be amiss to observe, that the plate engraved by Sherwin, after a painting by Dance, is a most excellent likeness of Captain Cook; and more to be valued, as it is the only one I have seen that bears any resemblance to him.

Observations, Respecting the Introduction of the Venereal Disease into the Sandwich Islands

THIS publication affording a convenient opportunity, I embrace it, to offer a few remarks upon a subject in some degree affecting the reputation of the late voyages to the South Sea Islands. If we for a moment suppose, that they have been the means of disseminating the venereal disease among the inhabitants, the evil is of such a magniture, that we are induced to wish they had never been undertaken. For who would not sooner remain ignorant of the interesting discoveries which have been made, than bear the reflection of their having been attended with such an irreparable injury to a happy and uncontaminated race of people!

It is a point of dispute between Captain Wallis and Mons. Bougainville, which of their ships it was, that introduced the disease to Otaheite. And we find, that Captain Cook was apprehensive of his people having left it at the Friendly Islands. Without enquiring into the grounds of conviction they had in former voyages, I am strongly inclined to believe, from my observations in the last, that it is a subject about which they are very liable to be deceived; and that what is laid down as positive fact, could be no more than matter of opinion.

In the last voyage, both Captains Cook and King were of opinion, that the inhabitants of Sandwich Islands received that distemper from our people. The great deference I pay to their judgement on every occasion, will hardly allow me to dissent from it in the present instance; and yet I must be allowed to say, that the same evidence which proved convincing to them in this case, did by no means appear so to me, and I will endeavour to assign my reasons. When we first discovered Sandwich Islands, in the month of January, 1778, the ships anchored at two of them (viz. Atowai and Neehaw) where parties were sent ashore for water, and to purchase provisions of the natives. On this occasion, I must bear my testimony (for I was then in the Resolution) to the very particular care taken by Captain Cook, to prevent any of his people who were not in perfect health from having communication with the shore, and also to prevent women from coming on board the ships. That this humane precaution answered the intended purpose, we had great reason to believe; for not one of those who did go on shore was afterwards in the surgeon's list, or known to have any complaint; which was the most convincing proof we could have, of their being well at the time. We therefore were under no apprehensions on this head, when we visited these islands a second time, about eleven months from our first discovering them. We then fell in with two islands, (viz. Mowee and Ouwhyee) belonging to the group, which we had not seen before; and very soon found that the venereal disease was not unknown to the natives. This excited no little concern and astonishment among us, and made us anxious to learn whether or no, so dreadful a calamity had been left at Atowai by our ships, and so propagated to these islands. But the scanty knowledge we had of their language made this a matter of great difficulty, and rendered the best intelligence we could get but vague and uncertain. While we were cruising off Ouwhyee, I was told, that some Indians had visited the Resolution with that complaint upon them, and that they seemed to intimate, that our ships had left it at Atowai; whence it had found its way to this island.

This account, I confess, appeared at once very improbable to me, and rendered me very desirous of an opportunity to examine some of them myself: for I found the above story gaining universal belief, and felt somewhat hurt, that we should take to ourselves the ignominy of such an imputation, without sufficient proof of its being just. During our stay at Keragegooah bay, where we had constant opportunities of directing our enquiries to the most intelligent of the natives, I met with none who could give me any information on the subject, nor could I learn that they had the least idea of our having left it at Atowai, or that it was a new thing amongst them. This circumstance, added to the very slight reliance, which experience had taught me to place in any intelligence obtained from the Indians, through the medium of their language, confirmed me in the opinion I had entertained from the first, that the meaning of those Indians had been misunderstood on board the Resolution. An instance happened soon afterwards which convinced me, that no credit whatsoever is to be given to such information. We had not been long arrived at Atowai a second time, before an Indian came on board the Discovery, who appeared to the gentleman who first spoke to him, clearly to charge us with having left the disease at that island, on our former visit. As I was known to be an unbeliever, the man was at last referred to me; and, I confess, I was a little staggered at first with the answers he gave me: but presently, suspecting from his manner, that he would answer every question proposed to him in the affirmative, I asked him, if they did not receive the disease first from Oahoo; a neighbouring island, which we had not touched at, when we were in these parts before: the man directly answered, that they had; and strenuously persisted in the same, every time the question was put to him, either by myself, or the gentleman who had first examined him. Such contradictory accounts as these, prove nothing, but our ignorance of their language, and consequently, how apt we are to be misled in enquiries of this sort. I never put any confidence in them myself, and have often been surprized to see others put so much. Yet those who have maintained that we left the disease at Sandwich Islands, have no better foundation than this, to rest their opinion upon. Whether it be sufficient to support such an accusation, I will leave others to judge, after what I have related above; and proceed to point out such other circumstances as tend to prove, that the disease was not left at these islands by our ships. From every thing we could learn, it appeared, that there is but little intercourse between Atowai and the islands to windward, especially Ouwhyee, which is about fifty leagues distant: and the nearest to Atowai, which is Oahoo, is five and twenty leagues. There is generally some misunderstanding between them, and, excepting for hostile purposes, the inhabitants rarely visit each other. But were we even to allow, that there is a frequent intercourse between them, which from the distance alone is highly improbable, yet it is hardly possible, that the disease should have spread so far, and so universally, as we found it at Ouwhyee, in the short space of time which intervened between our first and second visit to the Sandwich Islands. On the same supposition, it will appear very extraordinary, that we should have found it more common by far at Ouwhyee than at Atowai, the place where we are supposed to have first left it. That this was the case, however, from my situation at that time, as surgeon of the Discovery, I am able to pronounce with some certainty. The priests pretended to be expert at curing it, and seemed to have an established mode of treatment; which by no means implied, that it was a recent complaint among them, much less that it was introduced only a few months before.

Whence, or at what time, the inhabitants of these islands received disease, or whether or not it be indigenous among them, is what I do not pretend even to guess: but from the circumstances above-mentioned, I think myself warranted in saying, that there are by no means sufficient proofs of our having first introduced it; but that, on the contrary, there is every reason to believe, that they were afflicted with it before we discovered those islands.

Notes

[1]   That is, the official publication of the third voyage: James Cook and James King, *A Voyage to the Pacific Ocean, undertaken by the Command of His Majesty for making discoveries in the Northern Hemisphere, to determine the position and extent*

of the west side of North America; its distance from Asia; and the practicability of a northern passage to Europe . . . (London: W. and A. Strahan for G. Nicol and T. Cadell, 1784). For the imputation of rashness, see 'David Samwell: Pacific ethnographer and historian', above.

2   James King suffered from consumption and went to Nice for his health in 1783; he died there in October 1784.

3   Presumably this cites Kippis's encouragement.

4   That is, Kealakekua Bay, Hawai'i. See the Glossary of Hawaiian names. The ships anchored in the bay on Sunday 17 January 1779, and departed for the first time of February 4. See Beaglehole, *Journals*, pp. 490–525, for Cook's and King's accounts of this period; and *Journals*, pp. 1155–89, for Samwell's journal and observations. There are, of course, a range of other published and un-published accounts.

5   Other sources make it clear that some coolness on the part of the Hawaiians was immediately apparent. See e.g. Beaglehole, *Journals*, p. 528 and n.3. Possibly Samwell passes over this because he is concerned to emphasize the 'accidental' and entirely unexpected character of the violence, and, by implication, that Cook took as many precautions as he could reasonably have been expected to have done.

6   Kalani'opu'u (–1782) was the ruling king. He had achieved pre-eminence over the island of Hawai'i in about 1754. Son of Kalaninuooamamao (ruling *ali'i* of Ka'u) and Kamakaimoku, he had begun his rise to power as a war-lord under Alapainui, but soon turned against him to fight for his own chieftainship. His primary wife was Kalola. It was by his other wife, Kaneikapolei, that he had the twin sons (Keoua Kuahuula and Keoua Peeale) mentioned in this account. By the time of Cook's visit Kalani'opu'u also controlled eastern Maui. See A. Grove Day, *History Makers of Hawaii: A Biographical Dictionary* (Honolulu: Mutual, 1984), p. 65, and Patrick V. Kirch and Marshall Sahlins, *Anahulu: The Anthropology of History in the Kingdom of Hawaii* (Chicago: University of Chicago Press, 1992), p. 18.

7   Kamehameha I (1758?–1819), a nephew of Kalani'opu'u, was on the beach during the violence when Cook was killed, and sustained gunpowder wounds. He later succeeded in bringing all the main islands of the Hawaiian chain under a unified rule for the first time; the dynasty endured until 1872. For general historical background, see Gavan Daws, *Shoal of Time: A History of the Hawaiian Islands* (Honolulu: University of Hawai'i Press, 1977).

8   Feathered cloaks – *'ahu'ula* – of this type were among the most valued and potent possessions of Hawaiian *ali'i* or chiefs. Feathers carried particular signifi-cance; as Anne D'Alleva has noted: 'Feathered garments . . . signalled high status throughout eastern Polynesia, for to wrap the body in feathers was to liken it to the feathered bodies of the gods.' These cloaks were worn on occasions when displays of power were desired – ceremonies of state or on going to war. They were ceremonial gifts of the most exalted value. Red and yellow feathers were the most prized, being the most sacred colours. Anne D'Alleva explains that the feathers for the cloak given to Cook by the paramount title-holder of Hawai'i in 1779 'were gathered as part of the tribute paid by the common people to the elite each year during the *makahiki* season '. Anne D'Alleva, *Art of the Pacific* (London: Everyman, 1998), p. 107.

9   This was done on the southern shore, near Hikiau, separated by a cliff from the village of Ka'awaloa.

10   Ka'awaloa was the settlement of the reigning *ali'i* of the island of Hawai'i, located at the northern end of Kealakekua Bay. The village was occupied until around the 1940s, and there are extensive stone walls and other remains in the vicinity of the monument to Cook. James King, among others, understood that there was a degree of antagonism between the chiefs of Ka'awaloa and the priests associated with Lono based around the temple or *heiau* of Hikiau, on the southern shore of Kealakekua Bay.

11   The best account of this incident is that of Thomas Edgar, printed in Beaglehole, *Journals*, pp. 1359–60. Among others involved was the midshipman George Vancouver, later in command of the famous expedition that extended Cook's work on the American north-west coast.

12   Samwell's translation is literal.

13   This scar was not in fact the result of fighting, but of the accidental explosion of a powder horn during Cook's Newfoundland survey in August 1764 (Beaglehole, *Life*, p. 80).

14   The boat had been deliberately submerged in order to prevent timbers warping in the heat.

15   During Cook's first voyage he had twice taken Tahitian *ari'i*, including Purea and Tuteha, hostage (Beaglehole, *Journals*, I, pp. 87–8, 114–6); during the third voyage he held the Raiatean 'princess' Poetua and others, and more briefly detained the Tongan paramount, Paulaho (*Journals*, III, pp. 134, 248–51). These strategies may have been 'successful' but they also certainly produced great alarm and trauma that could easily have sparked wider violence in any one of the preceding instances.

16   Samwell's account may be compared with those of Phillips, Clerke and King: Beaglehole, *Journals*, pp. 533–51. Rupert T. Gould, 'Some unpublished accounts of Cook's death', *Mariners Mirror*, 14 (1928), pp. 301–19, reproduces fuller extracts from certain logs than Beaglehole, and instances the propensity to blame Williamson.

17   Cook was in fact born on 27 October, 1728.

18   Walker's house, in which Cook intermittently resided, with other apprentices, is in Grape Lane and is now the Captain Cook Memorial Museum. For Cook's early maritime experience, see Beaglehole, *Life*, chs 1–3.

19   The introduction of goats, sheep and cattle to Polynesia was a subordinate but significant aim of Cook's final voyage; as an expression of humanity and benevolence it was especially important to Cook himself. See Thomas, *Discoveries*.

The correspondence of David Samwell

To Matthew Gregson,
Upholsterer,
Liverpool

London. Dec 9th 1775

Honest Matt,
           I declared it for downright Cambrian Verity that some lazy dæmon or other has waved his torpid pinions over my head for these few months past, & instilled some juice more benumbing than that of the poppy, into my brain for never do I remember to have found myself so listless and averse to scribblings; I can assure you that at this present time I feel the influence of that dæmon (which I suppose you will christen by the goodly name of dulness) as much as I did when I wrote the following lines at the time when you had the disturbances at Liverpool which I send to convince you that you have not been out of my kind remembrance tho' I have not been able to write to you

> 'Ye Powers who make ingenious Men your Care
> Protect young Gregson in the Seamen's War
> When Clubs & Sticks in furious Conflict meet
> And Shouts of War are heard in Castle Street
> When Ocean's Sons in dreadful order range
> And threaten Havock to the proud Exchange
> May he innoxious through the Battle steer
> While all the boys cry clear the way there! clear!
> At his Approach may every blust'ring Son
> Of Neptune tremble and submit or run
> Nor send him from the Charming maid he loves
> To court the Sea Nymphs in the Choral Groves.'

I have been much delighted with the accounts of your journey & cou'd have wished myself along with you especially to see Cromwell's letters.

It it was convenient I cou'd like to take a trip with you this Christmas to the Land of the Leeks – if you go I have no occasion to recommend you to my Mother but I cou'd wish you to be acquainted with Mr Jones Assistant to Mr Owen the Apothecary, he is a very good natur'd young fellow, –

Give my respects to him & he will introduce you amongst all the young genius's there & you will pass a jovial Christmas.

I have some thoughts of going in the Resolution on her next voyage round the World – I have been examined at Surgeon's Hall & pass'd muster – and Mr Crosier, who is acquainted with the Captn.[1] has bespoke a Surgeon's Mate's Birth [sic] for me so that I think I am pretty sure of going – & I wish she wou'd sett off, but these American Affairs taking up so much attention I suppose keep her back – About 2 months ago I expected to have gone before this time – I am glad to find that you are so loyal at Liverpool, as I understand from you that there are 5 to one for maintaining the supremacy of Great Britain over her Colonies – I might have said Patriotic instead of loyal but that the word is so prostituted at this time that it bears a meaning diametrically opposite to its true Import, and is only applied to a Faction whose chief aim is, in my opinion, by any means to come in for the loaves and fishes, and which will stick at nothing to gain its' ends, not even at the total ruin of the Empire – As you know I was a flaming Patriot a while ago perhaps you may think that a place or pension has work'd my conversion, but may I accept of a place or pension in the higher regions from a Methodist parson if I have palmed a single Tester[2] – or if aught hath worked my reformation, but a persuasion, (not indeed from positive Knowledge) that the present Administration mean well to this Country in particular & to the legal Liberty of its several Dependencies –

I understand by your Letter that your Bro[r]. is not well, which I am sorry to hear – Mr Jones has never heard a syllable from his son therefore wou'd be glad to know in what manner he left the Ship – ill or well & for what reason. – I hope your father & all his family are well, not excepting his son Matthew – I have now the pleasure frequently of the company of our worthy fr[d]. Mr Gregory[3], who is certainly a very ingenious & sensible young fellow – & I am sorry that I am likel[y] . . . loose him soon as he is going to Portu[gal?] . . ..

D[r]. Matt I hope you will soon be so good as to excuse my negligence once more & let me hear from you before Christmas which will oblige –

Yr. Fr[d].,
David Samwell

How came you to spell my name after Israelitish Fashion.
My respects to Mr Christie.

Letter 11

Mr Matth. Gregson Upholsterer
Castle Street,
Liverpool

London, Feby. 23 1776

Honest Matt,

If ever I happen to be so unlucky as to neglect answering your letters for any considerable time you are sure to pay me in my own coin & very often with interest along with it. Tho' I cant say but it is just that I should suffer from my negligence yet I always think the punishment very hard when you inflict it with such a heavy hand & I am sorry that I am not in the humor to make you undergo the pennance of wading through an ample sheet of my original dulness – I make no doubt but to peruse such a sheet wou'd be more penal to you than to stand arrayed a la mode de penitents before a pious congregation of old women in Church to make atonement for your misdoings. My will is good but this sheet of paper is short.

You have seen in the papers that the Resolution Captain Cooke is put in Commission[4] & I have the pleasure to inform you of my being appointed Surgeon's Mate of her. I am in pay now, but shall stay with Mr Crosier as long as I can, I don't suppose we shall sail this month or six weeks to come I must remind you that in my last I desired to have a further account of Mr Jones the Carpenter of the Hector How is your Brother? As for yourself, I expect to hear that you are about launching your Bark upon the Ocean of Matrimony for in your last you gave an account how you had been parading away with a couple of Angels from Warrington & you threw out sarcasms at me for not being as you judged from my letter, a Man of Gallantry like yourself – if you are going to steer your course upon that perilous Main I heartily wish you a happy & prosperous voyage.

I shou'd have wrote to Mr Christie but that I know you will inform him of my proceedings & can present my respects to him & Mrs Christie better than I can. If he has done with Eachard[5] & you have no desire of perusing him I shou'd be glad to have him to take along with me, shou'd you or Mr C meet with an opportunity of sending him so that he might be here within a month.

When you write to Gloucester will you greet Mr Holstein in my name.

I have not receiv'd a line from Mr Gregory since he left the Downs. While he staid in London he was a constant Orator at the Robin Hood & the two other speaking societys, at every one of which he receiv'd universal applause I thought for my part that he spoke extreamly well, especially considering he was but a beginner – for tho' practice will never make him a good speaker who was not born one, yet use & habit have a great sha[re] in qualifying a Man to deliver him[self] well in public. & a good front is like-wise absolutely necessary, for my part, was I ever so well qualified, I cou'd as soon fly as speak in those Societies –

You will let me hear from you as soon as you can & let me know what sort of an orator you are

I am your affectionate friend,
David Samwell

Letter 12

To Matth Gregson
Upholsterer in Castle Street
Liverpool

London March 25th 1776

Honest Matt,

I found by the date of your last letter that it was sent on the very day that I put mine into the Post Office – so that we have both been waiting for an answer. however I should not have staid thus long without writing had the Ship been for sailing as soon as I then expected I find now she will not sail this month as least.

Echard came safe to hand the other day in which I found a letter from Mr Christie but not a syllable from you tho' I examined the whole book almost leaf by leaf.

I daresay Matt that you will rejoice when I tell you that I am a lucky Dog, for such I certainly am. A very fair prospect lies before me, almost a certainty of being made Surgeon when I come home – a voyage agreeable to my wishes – a better appointment than I cou'd have expected – for thro' Mr Crosier's recommendation to Captain Cooke I am made first mate & what will render the voyage still more pleasing, an old schoolfellow & countryman of mine is the 2nd Mate – the Resolution is a very fine Ship but the Discovery is but a small one I wou'd rather have gone 2d Mate of the R. than first of the D. Mr Crosier has been the best of friends to me & has promised always to be such while I behave well.

I continue with Mr Crosier & I believe I shall not be wanted on board till the ship sails tho' I have been in pay above a month & I am grown so much of the courtier that I can receive my country's money & do nothing for it without being at all molested with the impertinencies of that squeamish Gentln ycleped[6] Conscience – Now Matt I am damn'd stupid & have very little more to say till you supply me with a text in your next Epistle, which I expect quickly, if you wish that I shou'd present your complts. at the Throne of her August Majesty Oberea or any Message you wou'd wish to send to any of your friends at Otaheite you will please let me know in your next, who am D^r. Matt.

Yr. Friend & hble Servt.
David Samwell.

Letter 13

Mr Gregson, Upholsterer
Castle Street,
Liverpool

Resolution at Deptford
May 16. 1776

Honest Matt,

        I know that you think we must have sailed from here long before this time, & indeed I have been expecting to fall down the river for Plymouth ever since I rec'd your letter which is the reason I did not answer it before. The Pilot is now on board but the wind is against us. We are going a few miles lower down the river to a place called the Galleons to take in our guns & we shall stay there a week or ten days. If you will answer this letter immediately I dare say I shall receive it in London, direct it to be left at Mr Crosier's – I am sorry to inform you that your expectations with regard to my botanical splendor will be entirely disappointed. There is not one person in his Majesty's Dominions more improper & whose genius is so ill turned for simpling[7] than myself. Indeed you must expect nothing from me with regard to this voyage – all that I look for is the Main Chance – being made a surgeon when I return – your receipt for taking off the impression of butterflies I shou'd like to have –

The note to Mr Vivares I sent by an acquaintance being rather hurried always when I come to Town. When you come to Town my cousin H Samwell at Mr Rush's Goldsmith on Ludgate Hill will be glad to see you.

As to the female acquaintance I know of none but one that I care a damn for & with her I wou'd not choose to trust you but I dont believe you'll come to Town – I have rec'd severall letters from Mr Gregory – he likes his situation very well – Omiah & Lord Sandwich come to pay us a visit now & then – If Master Omiah's countrywomen are not handsomer than him I shall bring many of my nails[8] back – He takes a couple of bulls & cows with him & I believe he will take a horse – I find the wind will not be fair to day & I am just setting out for London so you will excuse this scrawl as the Boat is waiting – I hope we may not sail till Sunday as there is a fine ship of 74 guns called the Culloden to be launched from Deptford Yard just opposite to us on Saturday – Write directly

I am sincerely yours,
David Samwell

[In pencil on the opposite page:]

My Dear Honest Friend,

Yours I receiv'd on Sunday as by yours I imagined you expect to sail at furthest [?] this day shall make short up – The method of taking Butterflys as follows.

I hope you have a prosperous & happy voyage.

Letter 14

Mr Gregson Upholsterer
Castle Street,
4 Liverpool.[9]

Plymouth June 19 1776

Honest Matt,

We arrived here on Saturday afternoon after a pleasant Sail of three days from the Downs. I expected to have heard from you before we left London but as I expressed some doubts about the time of our sailing I will forgive you that piece of neglect provided you make me amends by sending me a very long letter upon the receipt of this. We were detained at Deptford 3 weeks by contrary winds, thence we fell down near Gravesend, staid there a fortnight where we had the honour of Lord Sandwich's and several of the Nobility's company to dine on board with Mr Banks and Dr. Solander; from that place we fell down to the Nore where we waited about nine days for the Captn. and Omiah. During our stay at the Nore I had an opportunity of going to Sheerness & Chatham & was much pleased with what I saw at each place; at Sheerness old Ships of War are laid up and inhabited by the Carpenters belonging to the Yard, about 30 families live in one ship & very snug too, I shall not pretend to give you a description of them, but can assure you that they are really very curiously laid out – at Chatham I saw some of the first rate Men of War which make a most glorious appearance particularly the Victory of 112 guns, and at this place are many more such as the Royal George & others which fill one's mind with astonishment to think that a Man can raise such structures. Omiah is a droll animal & causes a good deal of merriment on board. For my part I live as happy as I cou'd wish only that one's cut off from the Society of the Dear Girls.

Let me have an answer by return of post for we expect to sail in about a week's time at furthest so that it *will* barely have time to reach here before we sail if you send immediately.

I am my dear Matt,
Yours most sincerely
David Samwell

Direct to me – Surgeon's Mate on Board his Majesty's Sloop Resolution at Plymouth My best respects to your father and all his family & likewise to Mr & Mrs Christie.

Letter 15

Mr Gregson
Upholster in Castle Street,
4 Liverpool

Plymouth
July 12th 1776

Honest Matt,

Your letter I receiv'd this minute they are just now heaving up the Anchor & preparing to get under way so that I have but just time to thank you for your good wishes the last boat is going off presently Give my respects to all friends at Liverpool, my best wishes ever attend thee my Dear Matt I shall write you from the Cape of Good Hope; the Discovery is to follow us in about a fortnight

I am Dr. Matt ever
thine most sincerely
David Samwell

If I should never come back you must be a friend to the young Cub I have left behind at London, Dont take notice of this.

God be with you

Letter 16

Mr Matthew Gregson
Upholster in Castle Street
Liverpool
Great Britain

Cape of Good Hope Octr. 22 1776

Honest Matt,

             3 months 8 days   recd it 30 janry. 1777[10]

     We arrived here all hearty the 19th inst. after a pleasant passage of something better than three months We called in our way and staid three days at the island of Tenerife taking in wine and other refreshments – the Cape is a very plentiful country, & we live off the fat of the land during our stay, which will be about a month, then we shall set off for Otaheite where we expect to be about the time you will receive this letter which I imagine will be some time in Febr.y and March. I do not suppose we shall stay long at Otaheite as we must embrace the Summer season to try for the North West Passage. If we find it we shall be in England next winter. We have various opinions about it some think we shall & others that we shall not find it. Omiah is very hearty and I do not doubt but he will live to see his own country again, he is not such a stupid fellow as he is generally look'd upon in England, tis true he learn'd nothing there but how to play at cards, at which he is very expert but I take it to be owing more to his want of instruction than to his want of capacity to take it. He talks English so bad that a person who does not understand something of his language can hardly understand him or make himself understood by him. They have made him more of a fine gentleman than anything else. He is a good natur'd fellow enough, & like all ignorant people very super-stitious, Seeing on our passage here a very bright meteor pointing to the Northward, he said it was God going to England & was very angry that any one should off[er?] to contradict him, looking upon it as no less than Blasphemy – Whether there is any strange God come amongst you is more than I can say, as I have not faith enough to believe that Omiah is a seer.

I live on shore in a tent close to the town which is called Cape Town & is beyond exception the most beautiful I ever saw, – amongst the Spaniards at Sancta Cruz there was nothing to be seen but a pack of lazy damn'd Priests, but here we have people who cultivate their lands build handsome Towns & are much given to dancing and merriment, and if such people as these are not more agreeable in the eyes both of God & Man than a sett of

gloomy, bigotted, praying Priest ridden Miscreants then I'll be damn'd –
To day Capt. Cook din'd with the Governor at the Garrison 3 royal Salutes
of 21 guns each were given with the Toasts at Dinner, The Governor & all at
the Cape pay Captn. Cook extraordinary respect, he is as famous here &
more noted perhaps than in England*[11] My Dear Matt I do not know what
you are about, going on in the old Strain I suppose, kissing all the pretty
girls you can lay hold of and going regularly to Church of a Sunday &
dining upon plumb pudding like the Citizen in Pope

> 'a Joint of Meat his week day meal affords,
> And added Pudding solemniz'd the Lord's'[12]

Perhaps before I come home you will be the compleat sober Citizen
trudging to Church every Sunday with a prayer Book under one arm your
loving Rib taking hold of the other and a decent pair of Antlers branching
on your fore head such may be your fate, but for what I know the same
may be reversed perhaps your are a Buck of the first water & at this time
busy adorning the brows of half the Aldermen in Liverpool

Whatever your character you appear in I am still the same

> Yours most sincerely,
> David Samwell

You'll give my best respects to your Sweetheart or your Wife – to yr. Father
and all his Family Mr & Mrs Christie. I hope they are all in as good health
as their most obedient who never was heartier in his life –

This letter comes by a French ship which sails in a day or two. the
Discovery we left at Plymouth & she is not yet arrived at the Cape.

[Newspaper cutting attached to the letter:] [13]

> 'Extract of a letter from a gentleman on board the Resolution, Capt.
> Cooke, now on a voyage in pursuit of the North West Passage, dated
> Cape of Good Hope October 22d, 1776'

> We arrived here all hearty the 19th inst. after a pleasant passage of
> something better than three months; we called in our way and staid three
> days at the island of Tenerife taking in wine and other refreshments.
> The Cape is a very plentiful country, and we live off the fat of the land

during our stay, which will be about a month, then we shall set off for Otaheite, where we expect to be some time in February and March. I do not suppose we shall stay long at Otaheite as we must embrace the Summer season to try for the North West Passage; if we find it, we shall be in England next winter; we have various opinions about it, some think we shall, and others that we shall not find it. Omiah is very hearty and I do not doubt but he will live to see his own country again; he is not such a stupid fellow as he is generally look'd upon in England, 'tis true he learn'd nothing there, (but how to play at cards, at which he is very expert) but I take it to be owing more to his want of instruction than to his want of capacity to take it; he talks English so bad that a person who does not understand something of his language, can hardly understand him or make himself understood by him: They have made him more of a fine gentleman than anything else: He is a good natur'd fellow enough, and, like all ignorant people, very superstitious; seeing on our passage a very bright meteor passing to the northward, he said it was God going to England, and was very angry that any one should offer to contradict him, looking upon it as no less than blasphemy. – I live on shore in a tent close to the town which is called Cape Town, and is beyond exception the most beautiful I ever saw. The people here cultivate their lands, build handsome Towns, and are much given to dancing and merriment. To day Capt. Cooke din'd with the Governor at the garrison; 3 royal salutes of 21 guns, each were given with the toasts at dinner. The governor and all at the Cape pay Captain Cooke extraordinary respect; he is as famous here & more noted perhaps than in England. The Discovery we left at Plymouth is not yet arrived.

Letter 17

London 2d Febry 1780

Sir,

The friends of Mr Samwell may be perfectly easy about his safety to the 10th June last, as his name was not in the list of those who had perished by accident or sickness. No private letters have been received from him or any other in the ships as the Russian Officers took charge of nothing more than Government Dispatches which must necessarily be sent across the whole continent of Asia & Europe. They had lost only two by sickness & as one of these was the Surgeon, there is every reason to believe that, if Mr Samwell behaved well, of which I have not the smallest doubt, he will not only arrive safe, but that he will come home Surgeon of one of the ships. This I hope & expect.

If they do not stop in the East Indies they may arrive in six or seven weeks time; but if they stay to refresh or repair; they cannot be expected in England before May or June. About which time I hope you will see you friend well & am, Sir

> Your very obedt. Servt.
> Jn Crosier.

Letter 18

to Mr Gregson
Upholsterer,
Liverpool

My dear Friend,

As after so long an absence from England it cannot but be a matter of uncertainty to me whether or no this letter will find you according to its' direction, I shall only acquaint you of our safe arrival at one of the Orkney islands and that we expect to be in London in about a Fort'night from the Date hereof –

> Need I tell you that absence has not made me less than usual
> sincerely yours
> David Samwell

Fail not to remember me affectionately to Mr & Mrs Christie

On board the Discovery in the Harbour of Stromness
August 23 1780

Letter 19
John White[14] to [Miss A Blacburne[15]]

London 18th Octr. 1780

Madm.,

I was really unwling [*sic*] to put you to the trouble & expence of a letter, till I could give you some satisfactory acct. – of my having transacted some business of moment with Mr David Samuel, the Surgeon of the Discovery – The moment I heard the ship was pas'd Gravesend I hastened on board & met her at Woolwich, I had the good luck to meet Mr Sam[l]. the evening before at Mr Crosiers – who told me that he s[h]ould return on board next morning & would render me any service in his power, when I came on board was never more disappointed – as I saw but one baskett of shells & not a single bird – instruments of warr & dresses of the natives seem'd the only cargo they had brought not an insect, or animal could I find except one starved monkey. Mr S. told me the Surgeons Mate of the Resolution was his friend & that he was almost the only one that had any birds in the ship & that his were reserved for Mr Bankes but what duplicates he had I should certainly see, as soon as he came on shore & could bring them up to his lodgings. not caring to open them on board or expose em to the publick I've waited impatiently to see these, but without success as yet. Mr S_ has drank coffee with me 2 or 3 times & constantly promises that I shall see his friends duplicate Birds, & as to his, I may assuredly depend on. this he repeated to day but as I've not been able to get sight of them, and by his own acct. they were indifferently cured & by the length of the voyage was much decay'd – I ventured to purchase a few to day from a Mr Baily who had saved a few tolerable good articles, but being particularly acqtd. with Sr. Ashton Leaver[16] – he had the first choice tho' I believe this man had duplicates of most, & Leaver having displeased him. I got 3 or 4 choice birds in my mind from him – that I perceive Mr L. never saw. I should have purchased more of this Baily, but my dependence on Mr Samuels promises – Perplexes me especially as Mr S. tells me he proposes presenting you with several of his. I am sadly vexed I cant get sight of his, could I but do that I should know much better what to buy of others & every hours delay is injurious to our success believe me Madm.

You may depend on the best endeavours of yr. most obedt. Hble.

Servant John White

Letter 20

Mr Gregson Upholsterer
Liverpool

2nd[17]   London Octr. 23 1780

Dear Matt
         I make no doubt but that it has been matter of some surprise to
you that you have not heard from me since before this time; the reason of
it is that I have been so hurried and unsettled since my arrival here, that I
could not for the life of me compose myself for half an hour to write to
you or any one else. I am somewhat in the same state still, but expect in a
few days to have a little leasure to recollect myself. I should have deferred
writing till then but that I am afraid you would think I was dead or that I
had forgotten you, neither of which is the case – I received your letter &
one from Miss Blackburne at Mr Crosier's – Mr White and I have been
able to get some natural curiosities for that Lady, but I am afraid not near
so many as she might very well expect from such a voyage as ours – but
in this most people I daresay have been disappointed, for very few natural
curiosities have been brought home; there were not above 3 or 4 persons
in the two ships who made any collection of that sort, from the great
length of voyage great part of those have been destroyed one way or other
– as to artificial curiosities we were not so badly off but I understood from
Mr White that Miss Blackburne wanted nothing in that way – I received a
polite letter from her which I intend to acknowledge.

You must know Matt that Geography has been the grand object of our
voyage – there we shine – that we shall not appear to equal advantage with
respect to natural history there are many reasons that prevented us which
I may give you some other time – In our account of the various people we
have seen their customs & manners &c. I presume we shall not be deficient.

If I did not tell you before I will tell you now that I was made Surgeon of
the Discovery by Captn. Cook in August 1778 this piece of intelligence I
know will give you as much pleasure as I received on hearing of your
doing so well in Liverpool – it was no more than I expected – but I can
assure you I never expected to hear of such excellent luck befalling my
good friend Gregory as that of being made a Priest according to the Order
of Melchesidech[18] – tho' many extraordinary things have happened since
I left England yet of all others I think this the most extraordinary –

and so my Revd. Friend
some Bishop
On thy Head has laid his Paw
and made thee Limb of Levi's Law

Well Matt, tell this Levite this Israelite without guile to write to me – Remember me kindly & sincerely to Mr & Mrs Christie & I shall be very glad to hear from them – as for yourself if you do not answer this immediately you shall never hear a word of Omia nor will I ever tickle your imagination with a description of the beautiful nymphs of Otaheite – Adieu, give my Respects to your Father and all your family.

I am dear Matt
thine
David Samwell

No. 6 Meard's Court Dean street
Soho

Letter 21[19]

Mr Gregson,
Upholsterer
Liverpool
Single [?]

London Novr. 1 1780
Wednesday Night

Dear Matt,
I received your letter just now, which has given me some concern – tho' Mr White has not been able to procure as many articles for Miss Blackburne as probably he might have at first expected, yet I never understood from him that he attributed this in the least to any inattention on my part, for he always seemed well satisfied that I did everything in my power to put him in a way of procuring such things as he wanted and I must own that from his obliging manner of behaviour toward me, I still cannot but think that he did not mean to lay any blame upon me tho' some of his expressions may perhaps be construed in that light. I have just now called upon him but did not take the least notice of his letter to

Miss Blackburne – He had some time ago some birds from me and shall
have all that I brought home which are not above six or 7 in any tolerable
order but these are all new – I introduced him to the Surgeon's Mate of
the Resolution who has spared him what he could which are about six
birds, I have procured him 2 Humming Birds from another gentleman of
my acquaintance. I have tried indeed to get him some natural curiosities
from all those whom I knew to have brought some home – D.r. Matt believe
me when I tell you that very few natural curiosities have been brought
home in our two ships – the whole of those few have in a manner been
monopolized by Mr Banks. I do believe that next to him Miss Blackburne
will have the greatest number of birds.

Mr Baily whom you mention was an Astronomer on board the Discovery,
as he had a salary of 400£ a year no one had the least idea that he would
have disposed of his collection in the manner he did – therefore I never
thought of applying to him and when he advertised them in the News
paper neither Mr White nor I had the good luck to see the advertisment
until the 2d. day of sale, I called on Mr White to inform him of it and
found that he was gone to the sale, I went to his house again in the afternoon of the same day but did not find him within, I was shewn a few
birds he had purchased and informed that Mr White wished to know what
Birds I had for Miss Blackburne that he might not purchase the same sort
of Mr Baily the ensuing day, I left word for him not to trust to my small
collection most of which was spoiled but to buy every thing he could which
he accordingly did – and this is the whole affair with respect to what you
mention about Mr Baily – Mr White seems to be an ingenious good sort of
gentleman and I mean not to throw the least reflection upon what he has said
in his letter for I am willing to believe that he did not mean to blame me.

I have all along understood from him that Miss Blackburne did not wish to
purchase any artificial curiosities or he might have had a good collection
of them – Do you know whether or not she wants a curious collection in
that way & whether she would think it worth while to lay out 100£ upon
it. –

I am angry with you Matt for saying that you are troublesome to me – do
you think it will not ever be a pleasure to me to do any thing to oblige
you? then why the Devil will you talk of being troublesome!

I have had but little time to myself since I came home – I mean to spend this
winter in London – between Dr. Hunter,[20] Fordyce,[21] and St. Bartholomew's
Hospital I can hardly los[e?] . . . me in London much less come to Liverpool

according t[o] your kind invitation & that of your sister to whom I hold myself much indebted –

Give my best respects to them and your Fa . . . Write me a long epistle as soon as po . . . and give me an Account of yourself an . . . let me know why you are not married [tear] Do for Godsake make Miss Blackburne . . . sensible that I have done my best to add . . . her curious collection, or I shall feel mys . . . exceedingly awkward tho' I am not conscious . . . that I have been any way negligent in th . . . business – and you will oblige

Dr. Matt
Your old Friend

David Samwell

You shall have no account of Otaheite till you give me a long history of yourself & your own affairs –

Letter 22

Mr Gregson
Upholsterer
Liverpool

London Decr. 16th 1780

Honest Matt
    (You have told me that you are so – and I'll take your word for it)
    The reason yt I have not wrote to you before is that I am so much taken up with lectures that I have hardly time to look about me – that too I must offer as some reason that now I do sit down to write I shall be able to afford you neither matter of instruction nor amusement both of which you have a right to expect from our voyage & was you here I think I should be able to gratify your curiosity – but when I think of giving you any of our history in a letter, the matter is so various & abundant that I am absolutely overwhelmed – with, what shall I say – confusion I believe – and unable to say a word.

You have heard much about us in the Papers I suppose it will be nothing new to you to be informed that we left Omai with 2 New Zealand boys along with him at his native Island of Uaheine – a Horse, a Mare, Goats, Sheep and a great number of Hatchets & red feathers made him the richest man on ye island – he was first landed at Otaheite & here he met his sister and the first interview between them was very affectionate – He was very well received by all his countrymen and I make no doubt but he will pass his time among them very agreeably the rest of his days – The natives of all the South Sea Islands Matt are a good natured humane and well disposed people, in my opinion much superior, to ourselves in those respects – the women are well made, exceedingly clean and have very beautiful faces, when we add to this that they are universally good natured and of a merry agreeable disposition & always possessed of a good flow of spirits – What the Devil can we wish for more – till we get to Heaven.

The object of our voyage you know was in search of the supposed N.W. or N.E. passage the non existence of which we have proved – we sailed along a vast space of the N.W. coast of America, at length passed through a strait[22] with the Continent of Asia & America in sight and were brought up by the ice. I wish you was here and I would my probe point out our track to you on a chart – We have made so many discoveries, that all yr old charts or maps of ye world are now of no use – You must buy none till our Voyage is published.

All this has been the work of Capt. Cook, after his death we did nothing but bring ye ships home –

In the Discovery of which I was surgeon above 2 years we did not loose one man by sickness – a circumstance unparallel'd in ye History of Navigation. We had not the least appearance of scurvy in either ship From the various nations we have seen and the discoveries we have made, I may venture to say that this voyage is the most curious and important by far of any of the late expeditions to ye South Sea –

I have seen Mr Holden[23] 2 or 3 times – Mrs Haynes' Note I presented to Marsh and Creed who could not pay it as she is before hand with them already. Her brother was Master of ye Discovery & my Mess Mate. I have spoke to him about it and he has not determin'd yet what he will do but this I know yt he has but little Money to spare especially as he has had some other Bills on his Sister offered to him –

I suppose you often have parcels sen[t] down to you from London, give me the necessary directions y^t. I may send you a few specimens of y^t. cloth of Sandwich Islands.

I mean to continue in ye Navy, and Dr. Matt I hold myself much obliged to you for the friendly assistance you have so kindly offered me. Every thing that I can expect will be obtained through the Interest of yt. voyage –

Miss Blackburne will soon have the remainder of my birds – Write without delay, and propose any Questns. relative to our voyage that you like.

I am Dr. Matt
unalterably yours
David Samwell

To your Father and Sisters remember me kindly –

Letter 23

Mr Christie
Bookseller
Liverpool

London Decr. 17th 1780

Dear Sir
      I have now before me your letter of Novr. 1st. I thank you very heartily for the sentiments of friendship you & Mrs Christie express towards me and feel much satisfaction to hear that you are both in good Health. Since I receiv'd your Letter I have often wished to write to you, but physical Lectures or something else have all along prevented me, Apologies of this sort I have constantly to make for my delays and I see plainly always shall have –

The letter you was so good as to write to me before I sailed is still safe, tho' I have been often tempted to burn it, because I never look at it but it reproaches me for my Neglect in not following your advice of writing a journal from the moment I entered on board the ship. However a journal I have which sometime or other I may perhaps have an opportunity of shewing you – in the mean time I must give you some account of Omai whose landing at Otaheite I find is the subject of general curiosity –

It was the 12th of August 1777 At day light in ye morning when I was called out of my cott to behold the famous Island of Otaheite emerging from the silver wave, Osnaburgh Island at the same time rising like a pyramid on our right – You may well suppose the satisfaction mixed with anxious curiosity that was visible in every countenance as we approached by slow degrees this new Cytherea[24] & of which we had heard such pleasing such romantic accounts from former visitors. Omai sat on ye Forecastle all day viewing his native shore with tears in his eyes. We had a South breeze & it was late in ye afternoon before we drew near the land, Omai cast many an anxious look towards the shore in expectation of seeing some canoes coming to meet us, at length we perceived them paddling from all quarters towards the ship they came along side with[t]. hesitation & the first question they put to us was, who is your *Aree* or Chief, we answered *Toote* (Capt. Cook) Toote cried they again well recollecting him & seeming much pleased – eh *Toote* said we again. *Maitai* (very good) cried they and immediately came on board – Capt. Cook gave them a hearty welcome and Omai spoke to them but these happened to be people who did not know him. but presently we were surrounded by a great number of canoes in one of which was his Brother-in-Law, their meeting was very affectionate, Omai now learnt some private news & was informed that his sister lived on the spot where we intended to anchor, but were not able to get into ye harbour till next morning – as we advanced in with a light breeze we were surrounded by a prodigious number of canoes filled with men women and children old and young rich and poor with Hogs, breadfruit and all sorts of provisions so yt ye whole was one curious scene of noise and confusion – Our attention was for a while was drawn to one canoe wherein sat a woman weeping & looking earnestly at the ship This was Omai's sister who had rose with the dawn to meet her brother with her canoe loaded with provisions – he beckoned to her to come on board, his heart was so full that he could hardly speak – he took her below into his cabbin while the tears flowed down his cheeks.

She & her husband staid on board all day were very kindly treated by Capt. Cook and loaded with presents on their return on shore at night – Omai was presented to the King by Capt. Cook and was received very affectionatly by him as well as by all ranks of people who knew him – we had brought two boys with us from New Zealand as a sort of companions to Omai & these were always kindly treated by the Otaheiteans who are in their dispositions hospitable, good natured & humane – we left Omai & the 2 New Zealanders, Tay-we,he,roo,ah and Ko,ko,ah[25] at the Island of Ua,heine where I make no doubt but they will live very happily[26] – the two boys were very much attached to us & wanted very much to accompany us the rest of the voyage & to go to England – Notwithstanding the terrible ideas we are apt to form of cannibals, which the New Zealanders a . . . I can assure you that these boys were very wel . . . disposed, truly good natured, & shew'd a warmth of affection towards us that made us all much regret their being left behind.

The friendly intercourse that I have had with the Inhabitants of ye South Sea Islands have interested me very much in their favour – they are a very happy innocent people and their behaviour towards us has been such as must ever inspire the warmest affection for them in every grateful and feeling mind.

I shall take pleasure in giving you such other account of our voyage from time to time as I shall understand will be any way agreeable to you and Mrs Christie – but I must beg you to excuse me if I shd. be longer in answering your Letters (as I have been now) than I could wish was I more at leasure than I am – but do not let this prevent your writing to me as often as you can and you will oblige

D^r. Sir yrs unalterably
David Samwell

& know yt. I was appointed surgeon of the discovery in August 1778 – In that ship we did not loose one man by sickness the whole voyage

Letter 24

Mr Gregson, Upholsterer
Castle Street
Liverpool.

London Febr. 5th 1781.

Dear Matt,

       I dont know what you may think of me, but this I can I tell you that I am not dead nor unmindful of my old *Tayo*[27] – but still, tho' I have not entirely taken my leave of this world, it is only now and then that I can be said to be in ye land of ye living, for most of my time is spent in Dr. Hunter's delectable congregation of dead carcasses[28] – but this is nothing to you.

Tho' I know myself to be in arrears with you yet I have had the assurance to expect a letter from you for some time past – but I suppose you will say yt. you are too busy. That wont do. I must hear from you oftener and if yt can be any inducement to you I may venture to tell you that I am now beginning to recover my senses and am not so bewildered as I was and therefore for ye time to come shall be able to write regularly as whilom[29] I was wont when I could boast of being more punctual than yourself as well as of writing longer epistles wherein my opinion lies all ye merit of letter writing.

I confess yt I have been dilatory but it will not be long now before you shall see a little cloth from Ou,Why,ee[30] – among which will be part of a piece that was worn by my sweetheart Koo,è,hoò[31] the prettiest Maiden upon ye Island and perhaps you may be permitted to kiss the hem of the garment of Teroro the fairest nymph that Otaheite can boast – So much for that –

Tho' I never congratulated on yt. success of your gallant Townsmen yet I can assure you yt. I have sincerely rejoiced in all his triumphs and I can also remember that when we first saw all ye News-papers at China it was a matter of particular satisfaction for me to read of ye great success of ye Liverpool privateers and was not without some hopes yt my honest friend Matt had some hand in plundering ye poor Frenchmen

Tell me, have you had no share in ye privateering lottery, no French, Spanish or Dutch prizes fallen into your nett, I expect to be amongst them by and by – will you let me hear from you without delay & probably I shall be able to pick a Text out of your Epistle that will serve me to write a Sermon upon in my next.

But here Mr Matt you have accused me of not congratulating you on ye succes . . . of your Townsman at ye same time . . . You have not once deigned to rejoic . . . me on my promotion during ye voyage an object which you must allow was of no small importance to me as it was a change from a situation in which I could not get what you would call a Dinner once a fortnight to yt in which I lived in plenty. – & yet Mr Matt tho' I believe I have given you two or three modest hints in my former letter you have not once taken notice of me – Are Gregory & Christie alive I have been daily expecting to hear from them for some time past. Will you put them in mind of it and give my respects to every body at your Fathers. I am dr Matt,

Your old Tayo
David Samwell

Letter 25

Mr Gregson, Upholsterer,
Castle Street
Liverpool

London, Febry. 26th 1781

Old Tayo,
          Your last has afforded me much consolation, for I find that yt.
let ye 'Error of my way' be ever so great you are inclined to look it over –
but I dont know of any return yt. I am able to make for this indulgence –
however I'll try to write a good Epistle, that is, a long one, be it ever so
dull; I believe I shall never thoroughly 'emerge from my Lethargy[32]
unless you will extend your Kindness a little further and get me admitted
into your long-headed Society.

Frank Holden I have seen lately, he tells me that you are fatter than you
was in days of yore tho' you have not shared of ye spoils taken from ye
French & Spaniards – You have some scruples of conscience with regard
to such matters, but I confess I have none at all especially when I consider
ye part yt. the enemies of great Britain have acted towards her – I was
going to say yt. I would make Prize of ye property of all our Patriots without
remorse, for I cannot help ranking those honest gentlemen among our
enemies – Yes, seriously & candidly, according to the best of my judgement
they are ye basest, the most treacherous of them all –

I am concerned to hear such a bad Acct of your Brother's passage home –
I hope you have received better intelligence of him since you wrote to me.
I find a sort of fellow-feeling in ye distresses of sea faring people 'tho our
voyage upon ye whole was exceedingly pleasant & such as I should like
to perform again yet we had many narrow escapes & ye sad havock yt.
has been made among ye shipping on our coast by yt late violent winds
could not but strongly recall to one's mind ye distressful situations we
ourselves have frequently been in – Many a dismal night have I turned in
fully persuaded & yt. on very good grounds yt. it was 3 to 1 against me yt.
I never turned out again – But such times are soon forgotten or serve only
to reflect upon now & then with a sort of dreadful pleasure – I like a sea
life very well and am now impatient to make one in the busy scene that is
acting. I believe however it may be six weeks or more before I enter on ye
stage – the small concern I have in Wales has some call upon me to go down
there, but I have little inclination and less leasure for such an expedition –

should I undertake it I shall make Liverpool in my way & then shall see whether or no you can show me any of your so much famed Lancashire Witches that can vie with the Charms of *Cau,ro,a,eivee*,[33] one of ye weird sisters who dwells in ye shire of *Ocona*[34] on ye island of Ou,why,ee and who by ye magic of her fine eyes fascinated away every Hatchet I could muster –

I delivered a few specimens of Sandwich Island cloth to the care of Mr Hankinson above a week ago so yt I suppose you will soon have them – there are 2 necklaces which I desire you will present to your sister with complts. I shall be happy if she will do me the honour of accepting of them – there is also a small bundle of cloth for Mr Christie & Gregory –

The savage present I have sent you is no great thing, had you lived near me you might have had more, but clubs bows & arrows &c. cannot be packed up in a Box – Tho' I have been at Otaheite and at ye far more libidinous Island Ou,why,ee yet Mr Matthew some parts of your Epistle were very near tinging my cheek with a blush –
        The *Paw*[35] of Koo,e,hoo which I may say with ye poet is
                sweet as ye fragrance of ye morn & chaste
                As ye pure zone[36] yt circles Dian's waist. [37]
Your meretricious ideas have converted into 'my Mistress's Smock Tail' – and you talk of elastic Beds[38] &c. things yt. I never heard of before.

However I am glad that I have been so lucky as to find you out in time for it has prevented me from pointing out to your profane contemplation the chaste Paw of *Coo,e,hoo*.

I really begin to believe yt. you are grown a Reprobate, for say yt. you laughed at my *Christian* way of expounding the Revd. Mr Gregorys queries – what way would you have me expound them in? Would you have me do it in a Rabbinical or a Diabolical way? – I see very plain Matt that thou art a lost Sheep – and yt is ye reason you herd with the long-heads whose wisdom is of this World and yt. you assist in forming Societies whose object seems to be ye worship of graven images – tho I dont like to enco[urage?] you in your wickedness yet I have sent you a young Godling yt. was formed at Ou,whyee & if you still persist in your ungodly undertaking (ungodly I say, for tho' these images are called Gods, yet I could prove them to be purely Satannical) I shall collect from my notes such remarks as I have Made on ye sad superstitions of ye Indians in paintintgs & carvings whose example you seem so desirous of imitating –

– As to my Journal – dont you know yt. we were obliged to deliver up everything of yt kind to the Admiralty – besides was it ever so much in my power to publish, regard to my interest in ye Navy would prevent me & there is another consideration yt. has some weight with me, which is ye injury yt. such a proceeding would be doing to ye family of Captn. Cook whose memory on this side of idolatry I honour as much as any one. His great qualities I admired beyond any thing I can express – I gloried in him – and my heart bleeds to this day whenever I think of his fate.

Till you put me in mind of it, I had forgot yt. I had mentioned a young cub to you – it is not living – and what has affected me exceedingly is that ye poor mother died along with it – My friends in whose care I left her shew'd her very degree of attention yt. I could wish, which is some satisfactn. to me – but still yt ye poor girl shd. be so unfortunate as loose her life continues to give me much uneasiness –

Excuse me dear Matt – and let me hear from you soon
Yrs. David Samwell

My cousin yt. you mention is still in London and I was surprised when he told me yt he had not seen you[39] – He married while I was away & is doing very well in ye Goldsmith Jewellry & Watch Business [?] and gave me to understand some time ago, for he knows I write to you, yt. if you sh[d] want any thing from London in his way at any time – he has no objection to be your hble servt. &c. Nature made him as well as every one of the Welsh name yt. ever I knew much of ye same disposition with myself, but his long conversation in business has made him as sharp again as I am – He can ask a man for Money with a good Grace[40] – Now this I cant do if I was to be damn'd –

Letter 26

Mr Gregson – Upholster,
Castle Street,
Liverpool

London April 7th 1781

Dear Matt,
       Till I received your letter the other day I could not guess what
was become of your brother, had he only stopped abt. half an hour the
morning he called upon me I should have had the pleasure of seeing him
– finding yt. he did not call again I enquired after him at the Golden Coop
& at Mr Hankinson's in Queen Street but could not hear a word of him –
however am glad to hear at last yt. he is arrived safe at Liverpool whence
I beg you will present my best respects to him but tell him at the same time
that I am rather angry with him yt. he did not breakfast with me that
morning –

Well Matt, what shall I say to you? You have sent me such a string of
profound questions that I can answer them no otherwise than by whistling
Lillabullero, according to ye wise example, of my uncle Toby upon ye like
occassions. [41] – To answer them all would require a history of our Voyage;
which I can inform you for your comfort will be published with all
convenient speed – however let me in ye meantime satisfy your curiosity
a little with regard to yr. queries.

You must know Matt that the inhabts. of Sandwich Islands are of ye same
sort of People as ye Othaiteans, the language is exactly the same, so is
their manner of preparing their cloth, but you will perceive that their
mode of staining is quite difft. – You ask whether they painted them so
before they were visited by Europeans – we were the first Europeans who
visited Sandwich Islands and I can assure you yt we employed our time
to much better purpose than teaching them to paint cloth – we were quite
amazed to see such an infinite variety of beautiful patterns among them
& many of them so like our cottons – the colr is a vegtble dye which they
lay on with a sort of brush made from ye stem of a plant it is all done by
the women – I have more than once been called a painter of cloth among
them when they have seen me writing & ye girls have very innocently
taken ye pen out of my hand & shewn me that they were better skilled in
ye art than I was for they thought but meanly of the confused irregular
lines I made – & they said I had no notion of any thing yt was beautiful

for I never employed any other colr. than black – they really believed that our writing was the same as their marking of cloth – I never remember to have seen them express greater pleasure & surprise than some of them did at my taking out a piece of this painted cloth of ours & repeating from it one of their own songs – they did not know what the Devil to make of it[42] & I am sure Matt it would have done thy heart good to have been in the Hutt along with me at the time – a kinder a more affectionate people than the natives of Sandwich Islands the Sun never shone upon – nor I dont suppose ever will – but I shall tell you more about them when I shall have ye pleasure of seeing yo[u] in London, as I believe I shall – however I am in daily expectatn. of being calld upo[n] I am much obliged to you Matt for you . . . friendly offers – but D[r]. Matt I am going agn with Capt. King, he expects a ship hourly, according to Lord Sandwich's promise – it will be a Frigate – Give me no more of your jaw abt. my merit & Mr Matthew[?] – the Commissioners have confirmed me on ye list of Navy Surgeons from ye date of Captn. Cook's Warrant which is a matter of some Conseq[u]. to me – but I'll be damn'd if this is not more owing to Captn. Cook's merit than mine – Let me hear from you witht. delay & write longer epistles

to your old Tayo
D. Samwell –

My best respects to all at yr Fathers.

Letter 27

Mr Gregson, Upholsterer
Castle Street
Liverpool

L6 [in another hand]

Portsmouth, June 5th 1781

Honest Matt,

I believe I promised to write to you before this time but as I had little to say except that I lived at the sign of the Crown in Gosport, you'll readily excuse me. Our Mess is now settled & we live in a family way on board the Crocodile in the belly of which I now sit writing this epistle; where Jonas whilom took up his Abode, but not being fond of a sea life he only staid there 3 days & 3 nights – he was a happy Dog & could live very well ashore, but if this Whale shd spew me out in 3 days I starve by Jupiter – so my pious friend let me have your prayers joined to those of Mr Gregory that the Fate of Jonas may not be accomplished tho' it has been begun in me.

The Crocodile is a beautiful little frigate but I shd like her better if her Force, which however is not despicable, was a little greater – we are almost ready for sea and shall go to Spithead in a day or two, – as we are at present designed only for the Home Stations it is very probable that we shall accompany the grand Fleet, but I shall let you know before we sail how the Lord (I mean Lord Sandwich) is pleased to dispose of us –

Portsmouth is the most extravagant place in his Majesty's Dominions – especially at this time that the Fleet is here, so if you had come down you would have paid dear for your curiosity – Portsmouth is remarkable for having the grandest collection of Sailors & Whores (or if you will Rogues & Whores) that is to be met with on any one spot of the Globe, they swarm like Bees – & Cockcades are as thick here as leeks in a Welshman's garden.

The fleet at Spithead Matt offers to the sight of an Englishman the noblest view in the world. I shall not pretend to give you a description of what I saw yesterday while all the ships were firing in honor of the King's Birth day. I am sure if you had been there you would have turned your Breech towards the French coast & bid the grand Monarch – kiss my — it must have made thy *ministerial* heart triumph Matt & given the spleen to a Legion of our Patriots.

The croaking of these Gentry is all my Eye we are strong enough to bid the whole world defiance –

There is a rumor here to day of Lord Cornwallis having gained another victory but that the brave Tarlton[43] was killed – God forbid that we shd. gain another victory at such a price – I hope there is no truth in this report, but that our Lancashire hero still lives to be crowned with fresh laurels?

Well Mr Matthew how did you get down to Liverpool & how did you feel yourself after your journey? – are all your pictures come down safe? You had better turn book-worm & buy nothing but books – but I am afraid you will follow the devices of your heart & neither give heed to my advice nor my example – here I have more books than I know where to stow & not one solitary picture except myself to adorn my Cabbin – and you'll say yt I am a pretty Devil to *adorn* a Cabbin – I will not dispute with you about that – I find myself quite at home on board a ship and changing the scene or a better air than that of the Town has given me more health and spirits than accompanied me in London but I am still partial to the great City & prefer it to any place I ever was in not excepting Oparre[44] the Metropolis of Otheite & ye residence of Otoo –

There are so many of us Circumnavigators on board the Crocodile that it is current over Portsmouth that we are going on discoveries & it is difficult to persuade even intelligent people of the contrary – as to myself I take very little trouble to set them right for I dont care a sous what they believe –

As we have not long to stay here I have no occassion to desire you to write with^t. delay – Give my best respects to your father your Brother & Sister & believe me

Dear Matt your old Tayo
David Samwell

[On the guard is written in another hand:]
6lb of Woole
John Eaton.

Letter 28

Mr Gregson Upholsterer
Castle Street
Liverpool

Crocodile off Plymouth Sound
Tuesday Morning Nov. 20 1781

Dear Matt,
            We are now seeing safe into Plymouth 3 Jamaica Ships, one of which we retook the 17th from a French Privateer, I therefore seize the opportunity of letting you know that I am alive & well & that the Crocodile has been with the grand Fleet most of the time since I wrote to you last;

we had one separate cruise in company with the Flora Capt. Williams off Cape Clear where we took 2 Yanky and one French Privateer, but not of any great value; – from this place we shall proceed immediately on a cruise by ourselves of the mouth of the Channel for the protection of the Jamaican Ships that are still behind having been separated from the convoy – on this service we hope to nab a french privateer or two as there are a great number of them about. Our stay is to be only ten days, therefore my good Matt you must loose no time in writing to me at Portsmouth where we shall arrive probably in a fortnights time or less & where it will afford me much satisfaction to meet with a *long* letter from you. – we can promise ourselves but a short stay there as we expect & hope to go with a fleet to Minorca. Tell me some news of yourself, your father who was very ill the last time you wrote, of yr. Brother & my two worthy Tayos Christie and Gregory –

As to myself I can at present only tell you that I am very agreeably situated in the Crocodile with Captn. King & the rest of my old shipmates, we are all hearty & in good spirits & as none of us made our fortunes at Otaheite, we are all keen hunters after prizes; there is nothing so pleasant as the chace of an enemy; when we are not so agreeably amused, we find no small satisfaction in talking over the eventful history of our voyage and are happy beyond measure when any of our old companions come to see us from other ships which they do as often as they can; no less than 17 lieutenants have been made out of our two ships; we are perhaps somewhat partial to one another, for it is an article of Faith with every one of us that there never was such a collection of fine lads take us for all in all, got together as there was in the Resolution & Discovery.

The boat is just setting off so that Dear Matt I have time only to desire you & every one at your House to accept my best respects & to tell you that I remain

Your old Tayo
David Samwell

Did you ever send to Wilbraham at Chester about the Books?

Excerpts from other letters

Letter 29

To Matthew Gregson, 31 December 1781.

In a postscript: 'N. I must insist upon your keeping your word in *not* shewing my papers to any one – one of the Surgeon's Mates of the Discovery is going to publish the voyage & Captn. King's will be out soon, so have a little patience.' [Samwell was sailing under Captain King at this time.]

Letter 30

To Matthew Gregson, 16 May 1782.

'Ellis's Account of our Voyage I have seen, but I cant say I have read it through nor did one of us on board who had been of the party, the language is good but there is no spirit in the narrative, nor is it by any means copious enough to be at all satisfactory. We all agreed that the greatest part of it was written from memory, he tells no lies 'tis true but then he does not tell you half the odd adventures we met with; it is an unentertaining outline of the voyage – Ellis is not he who went to Wales nor is he of that famous Country, he was Surgeon's 2d. Mate of the Discovery & removed into the Resoln. with Capt. Cooke for whom he used to write his log &c. He is a genteel young fellow & of good education & I really think would have been capable of giving a better narrative than that which is published, had he applied himself to it but I think he never thought of publishing till after he came home. – He attended the Hospitals when I was in London & intended to settle in his native county, Cambridgeshire – it will be some time yet before Captn. King's or rather Captn. Cook & Captn. King's publication comes out – The plates take up so much time – I forgot whether you ever called upon Webber to see the drawings . . . the most intelligent & most formidable opponent I had in these political speculations was Captn. King & I have not had a good dish of politics since he left us – he has a true genius for politics & is by far the best informed on the subject of any I ever conversed with – I admire him altogether so much that you see I can hardly ever refrain from talking of him.'

In the following letter Samwell says that King had tried to take him with him when appointed to his new ship, the *Resistance*, but that a surgeon had already been appointed.

Letter 41

To Matthew Gregson, 11 October 1788.

'If you remember I mention'd Mr Trevenen to you as a very worthy friend of mine. He commanded one of the Russian Line of battleships in the engagement with the Swedes. He is as fine a young fellow as ever I knew & a real loss to the naval service of this country. I have had several letters from him but none since the engagement – how he fared I do not know, but the Russians in general seem to have had the worst of it. It is a pity Trevenen should ever have any but Englishmen under his command. The English sailors alone are capable of doing justice to his own gallant spirit. The papers have said there has been another engagement & that 3 Russian ships of 66 guns were captured by the Swedes. He commanded a ship of that force & he perhaps through the ill behaviour of the damn'd Russians may have been taken – but I hope not. [45] . . . I long to hear something authentic & particularly from himself – Trevenen was with C. Cook – Kippis has just published the Life of Cook . . . in he has mentioned me more favourably . . . I deserve. You must buy the book it contains the best written abridgement of Captn. Cook's voyages of any that have been published.' [46]

Letter 42

To Matthew Gregson, 15 October 1788.

At the end of this long letter, Samwell writes: 'I have not room for extracts from Trevenen you shall see it all when you come to town, You will like it for I know yt. you have a Taste for Poetry – you used to rhime in days of yore – I will carry you to S^r. Ashton's Museum – I have the privilege of taking a friend there any time, any of your friends that you would wish to compliment with a sight of it will always find me at their Service . . . I want to hear that you have a son. As to me all my bearns are at Otaheite & by their bringing up I am afraid little better than Heathens.'

Letter 43

To Matthew Gregson, 9 June 1789.

'I will give you some news from Otaheite just arrived which I had the other day from my old shipmate Lt. Watts who is the last that has been there – Omai is dead so are the two Newzealand boys whom we carried there along with him – Watts made every enquiry about them & was convinced that they were not cut off by any violence but died a natural death – perhaps the survivors through grief for the loss of the first. I was very sorry to hear it particularly as to the two Newzealand boys, Tayweherooah & Co, coàh. [47]

Otoo King of Otaheite was once surprized by a party from a neighbouring island and plundered of all his property except a picture of Cap^{t}n. Cook which he fled with to the mountains. He brought it on board to shew Captn. Watts & such a proof of fidelity to the image of his old friend does him much credit and also shews how much respected C. Cook was among the Indian Chiefs – Watts said he could not tell him that C. Cook was dead . . .'

Notes

[1] This was Charles Clerke (1741–79), who had been promised the command of the *Resolution.* It was not until February of the following year that Cook was formally engaged to captain a third expedition. Clerke had sailed in the *Dolphin* with Byron, and subsequently with Cook in both his first and second expeditions. Beaglehole, *Captain James Cook,* pp. 444–5;

[2] Tester: a small silver coin of six-pence value. Dyche and Pardon, *A New General English Dictionary.*

[3] George Gregory (1754–1808). An Irishman who came to Liverpool to work as a clerk. He soon became closely involved in running a theatre in Liverpool. He wrote plays for a while before, in the later 1770s, he went to Edinburgh to study divinity, and subsequently became a minister in London. He encouraged Samwell to write his journal, and his friendship with Andrew Kippis probably led to the invitation to write an account of the death of Cook. See note 18.

[4] Cook formally volunteered for service on 10 February and his commission as Commander was from that day. Beaglehole, *Journals,* p. 1459; Beaglehole, *Life of Captain James Cook,* p. 490.

[5] Spelt Echard in Letter 12; probably one of Laurence Echard's geographical works, *A Most Compleat Compendium of all the Empires, Kingdoms and Dominions in the Whole World . . .* (London: Thomas Salusbury, 1691); subsequently retitled (1693) as *The Gazetteer's or Newsman' s Interpreter* and eventually going into two volumes the second concerning the non-European world, as *The Gazetteer's or Newsman's Interpreter: Being a Geographical Index of all the Empires, Kingdoms, Islands and Provinces . . . in Asia, Africa and America* (eighth edn, 1741).

[6] 'Ycleped: called, termed, named. *Milton.*' Samuel Johnson, *A Dictionary of the English Language . . . ,* 2 vols (London: seventh edn, 1783).

[7] 'Simpling: a gathering herbs, &c. in the fields, gardens &c.., proper for physical uses.' Dyche and Pardon, *General English Dictionary.*

[8] Samwell would have heard about the trading of nails for sexual favours, which by this time had been the subject of versifying: 'With nails we traffic for the blooming maid, And the ship's planks supply the dangerous trade.' Cit., Dening, *Performances* (Melbourne University Press, 1996), p. 154.

[9] The numeral 4 added by another hand, as also in the following letter.

[10] The times and dates here presumably inserted by Gregson.

[11] The asterisk has been added at a later date, presumably by Gregson. He inserted into the local newspaper an edited version of the letter up to this point, adding

only the postscript from the remainder. He also edited some of Samwell's grammar and phraseology. He pasted the cutting from the newspaper to the end of the letter.

12 Alexander Pope, *Moral Essays*, Epistle III, pp. 339–48: 'Where London's column, pointing at the skies / like a tall bully, lifts the head and lies; / There dwelt a citizen of sober fame, / A plain good man. And Balaam was his name; / Religious, punctual, frugal and so forth; / His word would pass for more than he was worth. / One solid dish his week-day meal affords, / An added pudding solemnised the Lord's:/ Constant at Church and 'Change; his gains were sure, / His givings rare, save farthings to the poor.' It is not clear how far Samwell was teasing Gregson with the parallel, but presumably Gregson would have known that Balaam the sober citizen became Sir Balaam, corrupted by Satan, who tempts him through riches. He becomes a courtier, an MP and pensioner. He rarely attends church, he marries a 'nymph of quality' and his daughter a Viscount, his son buys a commission and dies in a duel. His wife loses at the table. He takes a French bribe, is impeached and hanged. He dies cursing God. See Bonamy Dobrée, *Pope: Collected Poems* (London: Everyman's Library, 1924, rev. 1956, repr. 1961), p. 244.

13 This extract appeared in the column of Liverpool news in the *General Advertiser, Liverpool, Printed for John Gore*, no. 581, vol. 12, Friday, 14 February, 1777.

14 John White, presumably Revd John White (1727–81) of Blackburn, Lancashire, or his son, John. John the elder, a brother of the naturalist Gilbert White of Selborne (1720–93), was a keen naturalist himself. He was a correspondent of Linnaeus and also of the distinguished natural historian, traveller and antiquarian, Thomas Pennant (1726–98). Pennant was a generation older than Samwell but came from the same area, being born near Holywell, Flintshire, and educated at the school of Revd W. Lewes, Wrexham.

15 Anna Blackburne (1726–93), botanist, daughter of John Blackburne, was a friend and correspondent of Linnaeus. An accomplished natural historian, she built up a large and varied collection. She died at Fairfield near Warrington in December 1794. See *Gentleman's Magazine*, LXIV, 180.

16 Sir Ashton Lever (1729–88), of Alkrington Hall near Manchester, an ardent collector whose extensive collection was famous in his lifetime. In 1774 his museum was moved to Leicester Square, London. Dubbed the 'Holophusikon', it was open to the public daily, admittance varied from 2s. 6d to 5s. 3d.

17 This has been written at the top of the letter, possibly an indication that it was received on 2 September.

18 Melchizedek appears in Genesis 14: 18–20; he meets Abraham on his returning from defeating the coalition of kings under Chedorloamer, blesses him in the name of 'God Most High' and gives him bread and wine; in return, Abraham gave him a tithe of his war booty. In Psalm 110: 4, David or one of his successors is promised an endless priesthood 'after the order of Melchizedek'. Paul described the priesthood of Christ (Heb. 5: 6) in the same terms. These texts were interpreted to show that the priesthood of Christ prefigured by Melchizedek was superior to that of the Levitical priesthood as represented by Abraham, for the latter paid a tithe to the former. Samwell's use of the

phrase is whimsical rather than precisely theological. Sometime in the late 1770s Gregory gave up business to study divinity at the University of Edinburgh. Ordained priest in the Church of England, in 1782 he settled in London and became evening preacher at the Foundling Hospital. He was awarded DD in 1792. See note 3.

19 This letter is torn at the seal, which means some words towards the end of it are missing or incomplete. Tears are marked by: [. . .]. In some cases it is fairly clear that nothing is missing.

20 The reference here is probably to Dr William Hunter (1718–1783), the seventh of ten children of a modest landowning Lanarkshire family. William studied at the universities of Glasgow and Edinburgh. He left for London in 1741 to further his training in anatomy. By the 1760s he had grown in fame and fortune. Appointed Physician Extraordinary to Queen Charlotte in 1762, he became in 1768 the first Professor of Anatomy at the newly founded Royal Academy of Art. He was an inveterate collector, beginning with anatomical and pathological objects, and then adding to it mineral samples, shells and corals. He was also a bibliophile, building up a library of c.10 000 works from classical times to the present, and a connoisseur of fine art. In 1767 he built a lecture theatre, dissecting room and museum at his home in Great Windmill Street, London. His collection was enhanced in 1781 by the purchase of the collection of Dr John Forthergill. Hunter was famous for his lectures on surgery, which he continued to give right up to his death. The series cost seven guineas and consisted of 112 lectures, given in the afternoon six days a week for three months. His complete collection was bequeathed to the University of Glasgow, forming the basis of the Hunterian museum. Roy Porter, 'Medical Lecturing in Georgian London', *British Journal for the History of Science*, 28, 1995, 91–9 (94). Alternatively, though on balance less likely, Samwell may have been referring to his younger brother, John Hunter (1728–93). John Hunter trained under his brother, and developed a very successful practice and lecture series of his own. Like his brother he was a great collector and left a huge collection of anatomical specimens, which formed the basis for a second Hunterian museum, housed at the Royal College of Surgeons, London. He was an exceptionally gifted anatomist and surgeon and is regarded as 'the father of scientific surgery'. Either way, Samwell was in good hands.

21 Dr George Fordyce (1736–1802), educated at Aberdeen, Edinburgh and Leyden. Seeing the lack of a school of medicine in London, he determined to offer his own lectures in medical science. These were extremely successful. In 1770 he was appointed physician at St Thomas's Hospital, a post which he held until his death. An associate of William Hunter, he was a trustee of his museum following his death. He was also a neighbour of Theophilus Lindsey, whose Unitarian chapel at Essex Street Samwell once attended.

22 The Bering Strait. Samwell believed that it was most likely that Asia and America were joined but if not, the ice pack would prevent Arctic circumnavigation. *Journals*, pp. 1268–9.

23 See also Letter 25. Frank Holden was studying for the bar; he was a friend from youth with William Roscoe and was a regular companion of Samwell at this time. He recorded that they philosophized 'upon the comparative happiness

of a savage and a civilized and we seem both to be of our friend Rousseau's sentiments'. LRO., 920 ROS 2065, F. Holden to William Roscoe, 1 May 1781.

24 Cythera is one of the Ionian Islands off the coast of southern Greece. According to Greek legend, Aphrodite (Venus) first emerged from the sea at Cythera, and the remains of her temple may be found there. It was an island of love of mythic proportions, arousing powerfully contrasting attitudes in eighteenth-century thought. In François Fénelon's best-seller, *Télémaque* (Paris, 1699), the hero resisted the pleasures and passions excited there. In contrast, in Watteau's famous painting, *Departure from Cythera* (1717), travellers are on a pilgrimage of love. Samwell was in Watteau's camp. See Michael Levey, *Rococo to Revolution: Major Trends in Eighteenth-Century Painting* (London: Thames and Hudson, 1966), p. 62.

25 In the *Journals* (pp. 995, 1001) spelt Tayweherooa and Cocoa. Te Weherua was about fourteen years old and the son of a chief, Toka. Koa, son of Te Wahanga, was ten. Salmond, *Trial of the Cannibal Dog*, pp. 187, 318.

26 Samwell subsequently learnt that this was not the case. See extract from Letter 43. For a history of the boys see Salmond, *Trial of the Cannibal Dog*, especially pp. 373–74.

27 Taio was Tahitian for a party to a friendship contract, a partnership that involved mutual gift-giving and name-exchange. European visitors regularly formed such relationships with Islanders, and the word was one of the Polynesian-derived terms (like tattoo) that entered many journals of voyage participants.

28 Hunter's students were able to practise dissection on the corpses which he provided for them. See Roy Porter, 'William Hunter: a Surgeon and a Gentleman', in W. F. Bynum and Roy Porter (eds), *William Hunter and the Eighteenth-Century Medical World* (Cambridge: Cambridge University Press, 1985), pp. 7–34 (23).

29 'Whilom: formerly; once; of old.' Johnson, *Dictionary*.

30 Hawai'i. It was common for Europeans in Polynesia to hear the honorific article 'o' preceding a name as part of the name itself.

31 Ku'ehu. See *Journals*, p. 1189.

32 There are no closing quotation marks.

33 Kuloaiwi: 'by far the most beautiful girl on board or that we had seen at these Islands. She took great pleasure in admiring herself at a Glass & with all the Simplicity in the World cryed out "Waheine maitai aw", that is "I am a very fine Girl", an ingenuous confession' (*Journals*, p. 1158). Beaglehole notes that the literal translation is 'a beautiful woman I!'

34 Kona.

35 Earlier Samwell (Letter 20) refers to the 'paw of a bishop', paw meaning his hand, but here the explanation lies in his *Journal*, p. 1180: 'the generality of young women have a piece of Cloth which they call a Paw [*pa'u*] round their Waist which descends something lower than the knee, it is lapt four or 5 times round them and tucked in behind . . . certain it is that we thought this Paw had a very becoming and not an inelegant appearance.'

36 'Zone; a belt or girdle worn anciently by virgins about the waist at the time of their marriage.' Dyche and Pardon, *General English Dictionary*.

37 Shakespeare, *Much Ado about Nothing* IV. i. 58: 'You seem to me as Dian in her orb, / As chaste as is the bud ere it be blown.'

38   Possibly Gregson meant 'electric bed'. Either way, this is probably a reference to the activities of the quack sexual therapist, James Graham (1745–94), who designed various apparatuses for passing electric currents through his patients. He gained especial notoriety for his 'celestial bed', which was supposed to cure sterility in patients who slept upon it. This was housed in his 'Temple of Health' at the Royal Terrace, Adelphi, overlooking the Thames, which he opened in the autumn of 1779.

39   Hugh Samwel, 'Hugh Llangar', was active in the Gwyneddigion Society in its early years, and was president of the society in 1773. Leathart, *Origins and Progress*, pp. 14–15.

40   This was prescient of Samwell, for after his death his cousin, who had fallen on hard times, wrote a begging letter to Gregson. Letter 55, n.d.

41   'Uncle Toby' of Laurence Sterne's *Tristram Shandy*.

42   See *Journal*, p. 1187; Samwell notes that the girls came to realize that there was a purpose to his odd orthography.

43   Banastre Tarleton (1754–1833) was commissioned as a Cornet in the King's Dragoons in 1775 and the following year volunteered to serve in North America. He served with great distinction, gaining a reputation for skill and bravery, and ended the war a lieutenant-colonel of light dragoons. On 15 March 1781 he was badly wounded in a successful action near Guildford, where he led Lord Cornwallis's advanced guard. In 1782 Tarleton was immortalized on canvas by Sir Joshua Reynolds in one of his most successful portraits, now in the Walker Art Gallery, Liverpool.

44   Pare, a district on the northern coast of Tahiti. Dominated by Tu (later named Tina, then Pomare I), the then paramount chief (*ari'i rahi*) of the Pare-Arue and Matavai districts.

45   James Trevenen (1760–90) was a young midshipman on the *Resolution*, and for Samwell he was a kindred spirit, a great admirer of Cook and a bard who versified some of his experiences on the third voyage. He went into Russian service in 1787 as commander of a voyage of discovery in the northern Pacific, but was diverted into active service in the Baltic when the war with Sweden broke out in 1788. He died on 9 July 1790, following action in Viborg Bay. Beaglehole, *Journals*, p. 1466; *Life*, pp. 499, 588–9, 701.

46   Kippis wrote: 'The circumstances which brought Captain Cook back to Karakakooa Bay, and the unhappy consequences that followed, I shall give from Mr Samwell's narrative of his death. This narrative was, in the most obliging manner, communicated to me in manuscript by Mr Samwell, with entire liberty to make use of it as I should judge proper. Upon perusal of it, its importance struck me in so strong a light that I wished to have it separately laid before the world. Accordingly, with Mr Samwell's concurrence, I procured its publication, that, if any objections should be made to it, I might be able to notice them in my own work. As the narrative hath continued for more than two years unimpeached and uncontradicted, I esteem myself fully authorized to insert it in this place, as containing the most complete and authentic account of the melancholy catastrophe which, at Owhyhee, befell our illustrious navigator and commander.' Kippis, *A Narrative of the Voyages Round the World Performed by Captain James Cook*, pp. 330–1.

47   See endnote 25.

The poetry of David Samwell

Ychydig Benillion a gant Dafydd ddû Feddyg ar fwrdd y Llong a elwid y RESOLUTION Cadpen Cook–yn y Dehaufor–ar ei Thaith o New Zealand tuag at Ynys Otaheite.[1]

Mawrth 1af, 1777.

Cyn codi'r Haul tirion ar Wyneb yr Eigion
Rhôf allan Benillion yn union fy Nôd
Ceir clywed f'Awenydd ar godiad Boreu ddydd
Yn cyfarch Gwyl Ddafydd, gwiw ddefod.

Daw Cân a Llawenydd un galon ai gilydd
I gadw Gwyl Ddafydd yn hylwydd o hyd
Eisteddant mewn cornel, heb sôn am ymadel,
Drwy'r nôs efo Samwel heb symmyd.

Maccwyon glan heini a gawn yn gwmpaini
Un Davis, myn difri, sy ddigri yn ei ddydd
Rhai morwyr fydd heno mewn Nwfiant yn nofio
A Baccws yn llywio yn ben Llywydd.

Wrth gynnal ein Gwirod bydd difyr ein defod
O wîr barch I Ddiwrnod sydd hynod a hen
Ceir gweled yn hylwydd y dû Feddyg Dafydd
Trwy Râd y Pen Llywydd yn llawen.

Yn Llundain mae Telyn, a bachgen pen felyn
Ai Lais yn ei chanlyn yn Landdyn iw lê
Cyd seinio'n felusion a Gorddyar yr Eigion
Un Galon yn union wnawn innau.

At Iechyd Cyfaillion Y'Mrydain hardd wendon
Cwpannau fydd lawnion i hoywon Weilch hên
Y Feinir a garaf dros gôf ni ollyngaf
Gofynaf a mynaf gael Meinwen.

Rhôf allan yn llafar hir Oes i Huw Llangar[2]
Sydd imi'n fwynaiddgar digymmar o'r Gwyr
Drwy Grêd a thrwy Angred ni ddigwydd im weled
Un Dyn mwy diniwed dan Awyr.

Rhoi clôd i Sion Ceiriog,[3] fydd heddw fel Marchog,
A Myfyr[4] calonog, yn enwog a wnaf,
A hawddfyd i Gymro, lle bynnag y bytho,
Un môdd a gaf heno gofynnaf.

Ag nid yw anhebyg fod rhyw un caredig
Yn cofio'r du Feddyg da foddion y fau
Gan ddyfal wyllysio fôd pob peth yn llwyddo
        Ar Long syn'n mordwyo Môr dehau.

Er cynnal *un arfer* a chwi sydd yn Lloegr
Nid yw ar *un amser*[5] mae'n gyfer eu Gwawr
        Gwyl Ddewi mi gawdaf o'ch blaen, (mi grybwyllaf)
Ddwy chwaneg mi dyngaf na dengawr.

                    Dafydd ddu ai Cant.

A few Verses composed by Dafydd ddû Physician aboard the Ship called the RESOLUTION of Captain Cook – in the Southseas – on her voyage from New Zealand towards Otaheite Island.

                    March 1, 1777.

Before the gentle Sun rises on the Face of the Ocean
I shall pronounce Verses, my specific Intent,
Muse shall be heard at the start of day break
Greeting St David's Feast-day, fine ceremony.

The Song and Joy of one heart, shall unite
That St David's celebration may prosper still,
They sit in a corner, with no sign of leaving
Throughout the night with Samwel unmoving.

Fine-fettled Squires shall be our company
One Davis, my goodness, is merry indeed
Some sailors tonight will be Vigorously asail[6]
With Admiral Baccus at the helm.

In charging our Spirits[7] to our engaging ceremony
With veneration indeed for a Day distinguished and old
One may clearly see Dafydd ddû Physician
By the Grace of his Sovereign in bliss.

In London there is a Harp, and a fair-haired lad
Whose Voice accompanies it most fairly to its close
And in harmony with the Tumult of the Ocean
We shall sing here as one Heart.

To the Health of Friends in Britain fair ocean wave
Cups will be charged to sprightly old Comrades
The Lady I love I shall not forget
I shall seek and shall gain my Maiden.

I pronounce aloud long Live Huw Llangar[8]
To me the incomparable gentleman from Gower
Through Christendom and Heathendom I have never seen
A truer man under the Sun.

Give praise to Sion Ceiriog,[9] a Knight this day
Also hearty Myfyr,[10] I shall make famous,
And indulgence to a Welshman, wherever he may find himself,
The same as for myself is that I crave.

And it is not too unlikely that some kind one
Will recall the Physician 'du' and my good physic
And steadfastly trusts that all will be well
On a Ship sailing for the South Seas

Though we hold the *same celebration* as you do in England
The *time*[11] of their dawning is not the same
I shall celebrate St David's Feast before you (I should say)
By twelve hours, I swear.

Composed by Dafydd ddu.

Notes

The notes are Samwell's unless otherwise indicated.

1   We are indebted to D. Geraint Lewis for the English translation (eds).
2   'Mr Hugh Samwell o Lundain.'
3   'Mr John Edwards o Lundain, Fe fu farw Mis Medi 18, 1792.'
4   'Mr Owen Jones o Lundain.'
5   'It is to be observed that the Author when he composed this song was near the Antipodes of England, and consequently that the difference of time was about

12 hours, or in other words when it was the morning of the first of March with him it was only the afternoon of the last day of Feb^ry with his Friends in England.'

6   On the lines of 'afloat' (trans.).
7   In an alcoholic sense (trans.).
8   Mr Hugh Samwell of London.
9   Mr John Edwards of London, who died on September 18, 1792.
10   Mr Owen Jones of London.
11   'It is to be observed that the Author when he composed this song was near the Antipodes of England, and consequently that the difference of time was about 12 hours, or in other words when it was the morning of the first of March with him it was only the afternoon of the last day of Feb^ry with his Friends in England.'

The Padouca Hunt

AN HEROIC POEM – *Written in 1791. – (Now first published,)*
WITH NOTES, CRITICAL AND EXPLANATORY

In the year 1791, the traditional account of Prince MADOG having been the first discoverer of America, became the subject of close investigation in the Caractacan Society of London. That part of the continent where the descendants of the first colony are said to inhabit, is supposed to be *Padouca* – hence the name of the poem.

> In Walbrook stands a famous inn[1]
> Near ancient Watling street,[2]
> Well stored with brandy, beer, and gin,
> Where Cambrians[3] nightly meet.
>
> If on the left you leave the bar,
> Where the Welsh landlord[4] sits;
> You'll find the room, where wordy war
> Is waged by Cambrian wits.
>
> A table in the centre stands,
> Of ample size and round[5]
> Like Arthur's where the warrior bands,
> Of ancient day's were found.
>
> Or like a cockpit, where the brut
> Call'd man, doth oft resort;
> To urge the bloody fowl dispute,
> In wanton savage sport.
>
> Here men from various parts repair,
> And different hemispheres;
> Who breaths the dale or mountain air,
> Towns, villages, and shires.
>
> Some from the bogs[6] their journey make,
> And Corwen's[7] rugged, rocks;
> Some from the banks of Tegid's[8] lake
> Fam'd Bala's[9] dunghill cocks.

Old Llanfehangel[10] pours her sons,
And Nantglyn's[11] rainy vale;
Rude as the vandals and the huns,
Rough as the mountain gale.

And chose who dwell in Mona's[12] grave,
The Druid's ancient see;
Glyn Ceiriog's[13] blades, end those who rove
Fast by the river Dee.[14]

In Walbrook for the common good,
They meet and fiercely grapple;
Like wranglers at the Robin-Hood,
Or at St. Stephen's Chapel.

There various texts they talk about,
In arts, in taste, and learning;
And often solve historic doubts,
With classical discerning.

One moon-light night it was decreed,
To sift the tales that run;
Concerning Owen Gwynedd's breed,
Madog, his gallant son.

Who, as our ancient bards[15] explore,
And Histories[16] a few;
Found out America, before
Columbus and his crew.

Upon *that point,* all came prepar'd,
To urge the warm dispute;
Either to give blows, or to ward,
To prove or to confute.

Fully determined to decide
This long disputed matter;
Did Madog cross th' Atlantic tide,
Or never take the water?

See clouds of smoke from pipes ascend,
And, hark! The pint pots rattle;

Let ev'ry valient soul attend,
It is the sign of battle.

Lo Ceiriog[17] first upon his legs,
He sternly looks about;
The President for silence begs,
Then Ceiriog launches out.

As to the question now before ye,
'Tis all an idle notion;
Deriv'd from Guttyn[18] Owen's story,
And Penguins[19] of the ocean.

Of you, my friends, I must complain,
You have some wild distemper;
Not one who hears me can retain,
"A mild and even temper."

Ned Môn and I sometimes agree,
But Owen Môn's a lad;
Myfyr is not the man for me,
And Dafydd Ddu is mad.

The puny rhimesters of the throng,
I'm sure I never mind;
Tho' Glan-y-Gors to make a song,
With Daniel Davies joined.[20]

Twm[21] o'r Nant ai cant I hate
And Sherlyn[22] I ne'er heed;
The Berdyn[23] clôff I reprobate,
For he is lame indeed.

Old Jonathan[24] has lost his ground,
Drwy holl Ardaloedd Cymru;
One luckless night his muse was drown'd,
In a full pot of flummery.

But all from Wallbrook to George Yard[25]
Sion Ceiriog's fame is known;
Full twenty years I've labour'd hard,
To gain my bright renown.

But still the envious and the base,
A despicable train;
Revile me to my dauntless face[26],
But I revile again.

Younkers instead of crouching low,
Against me wag their tongues;
To atoms these O often blow,
By strength of leathern lungs.

Men milliners I always vex,
And keep the things in awe;
Grave physic sometimes I perplex,
And brow-beat wrangling law.

Of mathematics I am full!
When wrong the plan appears;
Of Mason's, builders, I can pull,
The house about their ears.

State merchants[27] I can sell or buy,
Draw tears from undertakers;[28]
Tobacconists[29] I Cut and dry,
Make bow the sturdy Quakers.[30]

Taylors[31] I prick with needles sharp,
And Scotsmen[32] lash with thistles;
I oft untune the menstrel's[33] harp,
And raise the furrier's[34] bristles.

With my stern brow, and valient look,
I rouse the soldier's fears;
I trim a shaver, baste a cook,
And work the farmer's gears.

All clerks with iron rod I rule,
If articled or hacks;
And unfledged parsons, just from school,
Have winged with my attacks.

Philosophy[35] himself hath roar'd,
When I have oped my chops;

The frighted sailors run on board,
The tradesmen to their shops.

Each in his way I strive to drub,
And live in great turmoil;
Nothing goes smooth, but when I rub,
The oilman[36] in his oil.

But as in peace I take no pride,
When oilman dares to stickle;
I throw the olive branch aside,
And souse him in his pickle.

Bold captains[37] of the cambrian fleet,
I often strike with dread;
I break my jest on all I meet,
But no one breaks my head.

Yet once I've trembled for my life,
Thro' *Creens*[38] mistaken fancy,
Because I've scolded with his wife,
And sometimes fought with Nancy.[39]

But after all my rigs, you know,
And maugre all my fears,
No broken bones have I to shew,
Nor any loss of ears.

Like *Cockyn Degwin*,[40] side-way cast,
I'm sometimes left alone;
None will stand by me to the last,
But Dafydd Dhu and Môn.

Say, am not I the Laurell'd Bard,[41]
The Gwyneddigion crown'd?
The Cymmrodorion's just regard[42]
With bays my temples bound.

A spurious race of bards unite[43]
The *black*, the *red*, the *lame*,
To rail at every thing I write,
And blast my laurell'd fame.

And tho' I seldom make a song,
In rhime or reason clad;
So cramp and lame[44] it creeps along
They cannot say I'm mad.

Let Dafydd[45] boast of Twm o'r Nant,
And Myfyr of his Walter,
Whose dull and crude poetic cant
Is worse than Sternhold's Psalter.

And there's another medall'd swain
Who dwelleth on Eryri[46]
He's hardly fit, I will maintain,
A poet's horse to curry.

The *Torgoch*, too, and *Ellis Wynne*[47]
Will often gabble rhime;
To write it down they think a sin,
It takes up too much time.

These bards shall crouch beneath my fame,
I'll now declare, to vex'em,
The great Sion Ceiriog is the same,
The same with Guttyn Gwrexham.[48]

Struck dumb with terror and amaze,
No one to this replies;
Some at the wond'rous Guttyn gaze,
And some lift up their eyes.

MYFYR.

Myfyr, at length, indignant rose
Full five feet from the ground,
And said, "The Jackall,[49] I suppose,
The question would confound."

We came to speak of Owen's son[50]
Who cross'd the Atlantic Ocean,
Sion's Bedlamite ideas run
Quite foreign to the motion.

He wants to fright us from our task,
With this and t'other *Boogan*;
But, Gentleman, I fain would ask,
Is not his name *Siôn Googan*?[51]

Yes; and a Googan he'll remain,
In spite of all pretences,
To counsel him is all in vain,
The man hath lost his senses.

His head's a chaos where no trace
Of order's to be found;
So obstinate that no disgrace
Can make him quit his ground.

For Guttyn I have no defence,
His flights no man could hinder,
He soard beyond the reach of sense,
Then call'd himself a Pindar.[52]

When Guttyn[53] made his bold essay
All rules he deem'd a bore,
So gain'd a medal in a way
That no one gain'd before.

To order, order, Ceiriog cried,
With voice and action wild,
Ned Môn declar'd he was belied,
But Dafyd Feddig smiled.

E. MÔN.

Here Môn arose – looking sedate
And keen through either glass:
"My friends, why should a grave debate
Come to this furious pass.

I've close examin'd every chart,
And sought through every wild,
In hope to find the very part
Where Madog was exil'd.

But all my pains were thrown away,
I could no vestige trace
Of these wild Welshmen, gone astray,
Nor any of their race.

From *Myfyr's* dreams and Ceiriog's rant
I strive to keep aloof,
I only wish and only want
Some sort of *legal* proof.

Has that been brought from either side?
No, surely! you'll agree:
Each from his course hath wander'd wide
Upon a stormy sea.

The letter which the Meddyg[54] sent,
And to this board submitted,
Contains one Truth self-evident,
He was by Bowles outwitted.

And following up so strange a plan,
He next prov'd more unlucky,
You all remember that *wild-man*[55]
He brought here from Kentucky.

Against his voice your ears were shut,
You judg'd him yn *Lloer-oriog,*
What did he prove? – he proved a Butt,
No bad one for Siôn Ceiriog.

Whose shot, directed at the pate,
Poor *Rankin* could not stand,
So offer'd to capitulate
By selling all his land.[56]

Owain o Feirion is a blade
Who well deserves a rap;
Some curious converts he hath made
By making of a *map.*[57]

On which, without a grain of grace,
He made friend Myfyr spy

Madog's metropolis and race,
Beneath a genial sky.

And with such stories kept him since,
All in a pleasing dream
Of being, one day, SOVEREIGN PRINCE
Beside Misouri's stream.

Where other Harams, nicely cull'd,
Shall bloom in distant Vales,
And Myfyr nightly shall be lull'd,
By Meirion's fairy tales.

To make the Sultan's bliss complete,
To please Padouca's Lord,
Thither *Caradog's* shall retreat
With this *Arthurian Board*.

More peaceful meetings *he'll* provide,
Complacent, mild, and still,
No *Democrat* shall there abide
To thwart his sovereign will.

But all in one smooth stream shall flow,
Wrangling and strife shall cease,
And this old war-worn table know
To end its nights in peace.

From tales like these, at which I'm griev'd,
This axiom you may draw,
That nothing ought to be believ'd
But what is prov'd in law.

Till that is done, and laid before
The sons of brave Caradog,
I'll deem these Maps and Tales a bore,
And ne'er believe in Madog."

DAFYDD DDU, FEDDYG.

Next Dafydd Ddu to speak arose :
"In public or in private,
I never learn, from Ceiriog's prose,
What 'tis the man would drive at.

Without all order in debate,
Bewilder'd and perplext,
There's nothing more he seems to hate
Than sticking to the text.

Just like a blind horse in a mill
He walks th' eternal round,
Gives you the same dull larum still,
On the old beaten ground.

And as to Môn's profound reply,
'Gainst Madog's host so mighty,
He may with equal law deny
My trip to *Otaheite*.[58]

Where, led by love's enchanting smile
Among the tawney maids,
We peopled more than half the Isle,
With Welsh and Saxon blades.

But as that fact is clear enough,
Wherefore my friends should we
Seek for a stronger, plainer proof
That Madog went to sea?

And in America's wild plains
Rais'd up a mighty nation.
Which in *Padouca* still remains,
Of Cambrian generation.

If I, from Nantglyn, not long since[59]
Could reach Kamtshatka's shore.
Why might not Madog, glorious Prince,
America explore?

I deem the oath of honest men
Of sacred truth the organ,
And neither slight the historian's pen,
Nor doubt the faith of Morgan.[60]

Williams[61] and Owen[62], to their praise,
From facts have us advis'd,
Traditions of the older days
Are not to be despis'd.

And that prince Madog and his train
Th' advent'rous sail unfurl'd,
And, having cross'd the Atlantic main,
First found the western world.

Where following Nature's simple plan,
In climes where Nature smiles,
They quickly multiplied the man,
Like us among the isles.[63]

You've heard the tales of General Bowles[64]
Who says they're there and well—
But if they are not —d —n their souls,
I wish they were in h—ll".

SION CEIRIOG.

"Shame! shame! cried Ceiriog, full of rage,
How dares the Meddyg tell us
That they went over such an age,
Then damn the noble fellows.

Bowles and Will Owen I detest,
With all their idle stories;
But Rankin's[65] worse than all the rest:
He in deception glories.

There's nought but fallacy, you'll find,
In *trailing*[66] Madog's tread;
A Christian never *taints* the wind."
Here Myfyr shook his head:

And springing with elastic bound,
As if to cut a dash,
Kick'd Arthur's table to the ground
With one tremendous crash

All further reasoning to prevent,
And bring on stormy weather,
He upset candles, argument,
Pint-pots and all together.

The awful sound Ned Môn obey'd,
Which fatally o'erthrew,
All against Madog he had said
As well as all he knew.

Ceiriog aghast the omen took,
The President lay dead,
The *Crindy* to the centre shook,
And all the wranglers fled.

Thus rebel angels, when they dar'd
To raise debates in heav'n,
Soon as the'l hunderer's voice they heard,
To hell's abyss were driv'n.

So seeking out the various holes,
Alleys, and lanes, of London,
Routed Caradogs ran in shoals,
Like d—d spirits undone.

All light extinguish'd to a spark
By Owen Myfyrs fun,
We ended deeper in the dark
Than when we first begun.

O! send to me a Poet's pate:
To Ceiriog, love of peace:
And grant henceforth that fell debate
'Twixt Cambrian Wits may cease!

                              Dafydd Ddu Feddyg

Notes

1   The bull's head.
2   An old Roman road.
3   The Caractacan society, instituted by natives of Wales, and so called by Mr Pierce, in honour of Caractacus.
4   Evan Roberts – but, alas! Since these lines were written, the landlord is dead, and the bar is removed from its ancient seat. *"Sic transit gloria mundi."*
5   Amongst the various proposals of names for the society to adopt at its institution, that of Arthur was recommended. A wooden idea, probably suggested by the round table.
6   Alluding to *Glan y Gors*.
7   D. Davies.
8   Sion Penllyn.
9   Tommen y Bala.
10 Owain Myfyr.
11 Dafydd Ddu, Feddyg, from Nantglyn y gwlaw.
12 Edw. and Owen Môn.
13 Sion Ceiriog and Sion Llwyd.
14 Jon Parry and others.
15 Gyttyn Owen and others.
16 Sion Ceiriog a strenuous opposer of Madog's story.
17 Sion Ceiriog and Sion Llwyd.
18 An ancient Welsh bard, who mentions Madog's expedition in his works.
19 Penguin being Welsh, and the name of an aquatic bird, common in America, is adduced by some writers as an argument in favour of Madog's expedition.
20 After the laudable example of Beaumont and Fletcher, Dryden and Lee, or Sternhold and Hopkins, these authors *set their wits together* to compose a song.
21 Thomas Edwards.
22 Edward Charles.
23 J. Jones y Bardd cloff.
24 Jonathan Hughes, the Welsh poet, of whom Sion Ceiriog used to tell this story with much humour.
25 Where the society of Gwyneddigion meet.
26 This is rather taking too great a liberty with a pleasant old friend; though it must be acknowledged, that bashfulness was not one of his great failings. [Samwell elsewhere noted that 'he was witty satirical and humourous [*sic*], a sensible well informed man but rather too violent in his argument', NLW MS 4582C, pencil notes to opening leaves – eds].
27 Consul Jones, &c.
28 Sir William Flint.
29 Mr Rowland Jones.
30 Capt. Wm. Jones, and Mr Tho. Roberts, lately become Quakers.
31 D. Davies and his brother.
32 Old Cluney, old Rose, and others.
33 The Prince of Wales' bard.
34 Owen Myfyr.

³⁵ A person used to frequent the society, who called himself in direct terms a philosopher; the folly and the arrogance of such a man, were fair butts for Sion Ceiriog.

³⁶ Sion Llwyd, and Edward Lewes.

³⁷ Ceiriog used to take great delight in roasting, or rather keeling-hauling, the masters of Welsh sloops, who frequented the Seven Stars, near London Bridge, in the Borough; those who have heard him, will allow, that he did it with infinite wit and humour.

³⁸ *Creen* (rather Crin) withered – a name given to the landlord by Keiriog.

³⁹ The bar-maid.

⁴⁰ The tithe division of hay or corn, – Keiriog one night at the George remaining in his chair whilst every one besides had departed, or was departing, Owen Môn very neatly called him *Cockyn Degwn.*

⁴¹ Keiriog was Bard to the society of Gwyneddigion.

⁴² The Cymmrodorion voted him a medal for his ode on the death of Mr Richard Morys. *Note* Elicidative [*sic*] of his gining [*sic*] the prize-medal, extracted from the works of a Celtic author of the present century.

> Like that great Bard yclep'd Sion Ceiriog,
> Who made an ode when quite *cynddeiriog,*
> To tell the world some high flown stories
> About the feats of Richard Moris.
> An ode that render'd *Myfyr* mad,
> And *Robin Ddu* declar'd too bad;
> A monstrous bore in Robin's eyes;
> Against his own it won the prize.
> This Myfyr thought was monstrous wrong,
> And damn'd Sion Ceiriog and his song.
> Yet all that Myfyr said and swore,
> While Robin loudly cried *encore,*
> Could not the Cymmrodorion hinder
> From crowning Sion the Cambrian Pindar.
> Myfyr, who was not well prepar'd,
> For such a verdict, stern declar'd,
> Those judges erred, like me, who want
> To make a Shakspear of the *Nant**
> *Twm, o'r Nant.

⁴³ The Welsh bards take a name from the colour of their hair, or other circumstances; for instance, Thomas Jones calls himself *Y Bardd Cloff,* the lame bard, because he has the misfortune of being lame.

⁴⁴ This is unjust. – Author.

⁴⁵ About this time Dafydd Ddu and O. Myfyr had strong disputes concerning the superior poetical talents of Thomas Edwards and Walter Davies, who gained two medals at the Eisteddfodau.

⁴⁶ Dafydd Thomas, who gained a medal.

⁴⁷ Two Welsh Poets, noted for extempore composition; but who, through an unhappy defect of education, were unable to write; hence Ceiriog's ironical allusion.

48 His signature, when he gained the prize-medal for his ode, from the Cymmrodorion Society. The C in Ceiriog is to be sounded like K.

49 A name sometimes bestowed on Sion Ceiriog by O. Myfyr.

50 Madog son of Owen Gwynedd.

51 Another Surname given to Siôn Ceiriog.

52 Siôn Ceiriog having, in his Ode, laid aside all the rules of Welsh poetry, used to say, as an excuse, that he had copied Pindar – in his own words, that he had written *ar Ddull Pindar*.

53 Guttyn Gwrexham.

54 Dafydd Ddu addressed a letter to the Caractacans, giving an account of his interview with General Bowles, relative to the Padoucas.

55 The Revd Mr Rankin of Kentucky, who professing to know some circumstances relative to the descendants of Madog, was introduced to the Caractacan Society by the Meddyg.

56 Mr Rankin, instead of giving a satisfactory account of any knowledge he had acquired of the Padoucas or Welsh Indians seemed only solicitous to sell some land, of which he was possessed in Kentucky; and which he offered to the Caractacans as a great bargain.

57 Owain o Feirion very ingeniously made out a most accurate map of Padouca, its rivers, mountains, towns, &c. and fixed their latitudes and longitude with great precision.

58 In 1777.

59 In 1779.

60 The Revd Mr Morgan gave early intelligence of the Welsh Indians.

61 The Revd Dr. Williams.

62 Mr William Owen.

63 South Sea Islands.

64 General Bowles, who had travelled over great part of America, and was in England in 1791, gave it as his firm opinion, that there is a nation of Welsh Indians near the river Missouri in America.

65 The Revd Mr Rankin, however, adduced several circumstances in proof of the existence of a Welsh Colony in America – such as the construction of old forts, and encampments, the ruins of which still remain.

66 Mr R. used the word *trails* for *traces* or *vestiges*.

The Negro Boy

Note on 'The Negro Boy'

Samwell was opposed to slavery, as was William Roscoe, but their friend Matthew Gregson was prepared to justify it, as were most Liverpool merchants. He used, so it appears, the argument that conditions aboard the slavers were no worse than they were for most sailors at sea. Samwell's response was robust and revealing:

> Do as you would be done by Matthew and do not oppress the poor negroes – You talk of Souldiers & Sailors! I can assure you that sailors in general on board a Man of War live as comfortable or more so than most labouring people on shore. I glory in a Man of War not only as being the pride of every Englishman, but that I have always seen the sailors well treated on board, well fed & well clothed. Your Guineamen to be sure are the Prisons the Bridewells & graves of British Sailors (Letter 42, 15 October 1788).

Poets were mobilized in the campaign against the slave trade, and the poets of sensibility showed that they were not devoid of a social conscience.[1] Samwell's friend, Anna Seward, had been asked in 1788 to contribute some poems to the anti-slavery campaign. She declined, but only on the grounds that so many had already been composed. Perhaps Samwell's personal altercation with Gregson over slavery convinced him of the need to keep up the appeal to the public. He was anyway, like his friend Iolo Morganwg (Edward Williams), in no doubt that the topic was suitable for versification. In the volume of Welsh poetry which he took on the third voyage, he later pasted from the newspapers, 'An Apostrophy on Liberty . . . extracted from Edward Williams's Ode', which began,

> Join here thy bards with mournful note,
> They weep for Afric's injur'd race,
> Long has *thy* Muse, in worlds remote,
> Sang loud of Britain's soul disgrace.[2]

In similar vein, Samwell in the *Negro Boy* enlists sentiment in the cause of anti-slavery, heightening the pathos by the preface, which conditions the way one reads the poem.

The Negro Boy

(The AFRICAN PRINCE, lately arrived in England, having been asked what he had given for his Watch? answered, 'What I will never give again – I gave a fine boy for it'.)

When Avarice enslaves the mind,
And selfish views alone bear sway,
Man turns a savage to his kind
And blood and rapine mark his way
Alas! for this poor simple toy
I sold a hapless NEGRO BOY,

His Father's hope, his Mother's pride,
Though black, yet comely to the view
I tore him helpless from their side,
And gave him to a ruffian crew,
To fiends that Afric's coast annoy,
I sold the hapless NEGRO BOY

From Country, Friends and Parents torn,
His tender limbs in chains confin'd
I saw him o'er the billows borne
And mark'd the agony of his mind;
But still to gain this simple toy,
I gave the weeping Negro Boy.

In Isles that deck the western wave,
I doom'd the hapless youth to dwell;
A poor, forlorn, insulted slave!
A beast – that CHRISTIANS buy and sell!
And in their cruel tasks employ
The much enduring NEGRO BOY.

His wretched parents long shall mourn,
Shall explore the distant main,
In hope to see the youth return:
But all their hopes and sighs are vain:
They never shall the sight enjoy
Of their lamented NEGRO BOY.

Beneath a tyrant's harsh command,
He wears away his youthful prime,
Far distant from his native land,
A stranger in a foreign clime.
No pleasing thoughts his mind employ:
A poor dejected NEGRO BOY.

But He who walks upon the wind
Whose voice in thunder's heard on high,
Who doth the raging tempest bind,
And hurl the lightening through the sky –
In his own time will sure destroy
The Oppression of a NEGRO BOY.

Notes

[1]   See John Brewer, *The Pleasures of the Imagination. English Culture in the Eighteenth century* (Harper Collins, London, 1997), p. 580 (Eds).
[2]   National Library of Wales, MS.4582C – cutting pasted on to the inside of the back cover (Eds).

Ode for the New Year, MDCC,XC

As it was intended to have been rehearsed this Day at St. James's

I

BRITAIN, for arts, for arms renown'd
To this wide earth's remotest bound!
As time rolls on successive years,
With ev'ry blessing crown'd appears,
And claims th'admiring world's applause
For patriot chiefs, for equal laws
Whose influence, extended wide, displays
In man, the image of the first great cause
    The center She from whence the sun
    Of liberty his course begun,
And warm'd surrounding nations with his rays.
Favour'd of Heav'n, the queen of isles,
    On freedom's glorious effort, smiles,
    To throw vile slav'ry's chains aside.
    And crush that antique feudal pride
    Which cruel, desperate and bold,
    Long reign'd in Gallia uncontroul'd.
But reigns no more — at lengthe dauntless Gaul
Reclaims man's noblest right — the liberty of all.

II

Like clouds before the rising day,
The gloom of slav'ry melt away,
And superstition fell and blind
Yields up her empire o'er the mind,
And bigot priests their crimes atone,
By bending at religion's throne,
Which he the Saviour of the world reveal'd
To breathe in man a spirit like his own.
    For lo! on Gallia, Belgia's plains,
    The radiant light of freedom reigns,
    From miserable man, alas! too long conceal'd.
        Primeval shades of tenfold night,
        No more shall blind the mortal[1] sight.
        The darkened nations from afar,

Shall hail fair freedom's beautious star,
Which now ariseth in the west,
And soon shall gild the glowing east,
Where man debas'd by tyrant laws unjust,
Before his fellow man still bows and licks the dust.

III

Thy age, blest freedom is begun!
Proceed thy destin'd course to run!
Till Europe's states, like Britain free,
And Asia's sons shall worship thee,
Till Afric's hords thy cause maintain,
And they beyond the Western main
In groves profound, thy frequent shrines shall rear,
Where olive tribes delighted hear thy strain,
Till virtue, peace and love abound,
And science casts her beam around.
To shew benighted nations how they err.
The muse's eye can pierce the gloom,
That hangs o'er ages yet to come.
All hail this Æra, first and best,
That bids futurity be blest,
Distinguish'd as the whitest age
Displayed on time's immortal page,
And hail to those, to whom 'tis given to see
This Year — the opening dawn of perfect liberty!

THE END

Notes

1   Corrected to 'mental' (Eds).

Ode

WRITTEN ON A LONG AND UNCOMMONLY
TEMPESTUOUS CRUISE, WITH A SQUADRON OF MEN OF WAR,
IN ABOUT 63 DEGREES NORTH LAT. DECEMBER 24, 1794.
BY DAVID SAMWELL

On Norway's bleak and rugged shore,
In concert with old Ocean's roar,
  I strive to wake the lyre;
Although these dark and frozen skies
Forbid the Man of Rhime to rise
  And catch celestial fire.

Thou gloomy Genius of the North,
Let all thy shaggy bears come forth
  From out their drear abode!
And let thy wolves, at midnight's noon,
Forbear to howl yon rising moon,
  But listen to my ode.

Around the Scald,[1] who rudely sings,
The half year's night her mantle flings,
  And wraps him in the dark;
The sun is gone his Southern rout,
Our purser's candles are burnt out,
  Extinguish'd to a spark.

While thus forsaken by the sun
We cruise for Frenchmen – or for fun,
  And dance the hays together;
The sport of waters and the wind,
No Sans culottes or fun we find,
  But winter and rough weather.

Ye Hags, in Lapland caves who dwell,
And boast propitious gales to sell
  To seamen for their riches,
Give us a wind for England fit,
We'll give you drafts on Billy Pitt,
  Ye sacrilegious —

We'll give, besides, the murd'rer's fat,
And finger of birth strangled brat,
         Untimely doom'd to die;
But, if with more regard ye view,
The liver of blaspheming Jew,
         Duke's place² shall that supply.

O grant us then to leave this coast,
Where we have long been tempest-tost,
         Depriv'd of chearful day!
The gallant sailor's spirits flag,
But not one foul infernal hag
         Will speed him on his way.

Then hail, NEW MOON, the poet's friend!
Our wearied hopes must now depend,
         On thy renascent light;
O calm the ocean and the air,
Convert this adverse wind to fair,
         And gild our polar night!

So may Endymion faithful prove,
On Latmos, and return thy love,
         Soft regent of the main!
And long unrival's mayst thou keep
The sov'reign empire of the deep,
And ev'ry poet's brain!

For me, of Cambrian lineage sprung,
Soon as I see thy bow new-strung,
         I bless the light divine;
And the first off'ring that I bear
Confesses thy maternal care,
         This moon-struck Ode of mine.

And, lo! Obeying Dian's will,
Auspicious winds³ our canvas fill,
         Of which the sailor brags;
Divining, as he quaffs his grog,
Those breezes—unprophetic dog—
         Were sent by Lapland hags.

But thy propitious aid alone,
Chaste Cynthia, shall thy vot'ry own,
Who like a seer espies
(When sailor's vision, overcast,
Can see no higher than the mast)
The secret of the skies.

1   'A Northern bard.'
2   'The chief asylum of the Children of Israel in our land.'
3   'On Christmas day, which had blown almost a constant gale from the South
    for above six weeks, changed in our favour, and continued so till our
    squadron arrived in the Downs – and let me add, this fair wind proved, in
    such a situation, as sumptuous a treat to us as *all* (down from the Admiral,
    who had only salt beef on his table, to the common sailor, who had nothing
    better) as to our jovial friends in England were the turkeys, chines, etc.,
    smoking *that day* on their boards. – Few ships have experienced such a long
    continuance of *unvaried stormy weather*, and none, perhaps none ever cruised
    in such high latitudes in the depth of winter.'

Glossary of Hawaiian names

Places

Samwell	Standard
Atowai	Kauai
Kavaroah	Ka'awaloa
Kerag,e,goo,ah	Kealakekua
Mowee	Maui
Neehow	Niihau
Oahoo	Oahu
Ou,why.ee	Hawai'i

People

Samwell	Standard
Coho	Koho (chief of Kona district, Hawai'i)
Coo,aha	Koa (priest of Hawai'i)
Ka,mea,mea	Kamehameha (chief of Hawai'i, later the paramount chief of the Hawaiian islands)
Kaneekapo,herei	Kaneikapolei (female chief, wife of Kalaniopu'u)
Kanynah	Kana'ina (chief, d.14 Feb. 1779)
Kaireekea	Keli'ikea (priest)
Kareemoo	Kalimu (chief, d.14 Feb. 1779)
Karimano,craha	Kalima-nou-ka-'aha (chief)
Kariopoo	Kalani'opu'u (paramount chief of Hawai'i)
Keowa	Keoua (younger son of Kalani'opu'u)
Koohowrooah	Kuakahela (one of Kana'ina's three brothers)
Mahowra	Mahole (short for Kamaholelani, relative of Kamakahelei of Kauai)
Nooah	Nu'a (relation of Kalani'opu'u, said to have stabbed Cook)

Omea	Omeeah (priest of Kealakekua Bay, Hawai'i, associated with the god Lono)
Ore,reemo,horanee	Lelemahoalani (daughter of Kamakahelei of Kauai)
Oteeha	Kiha (former husband of Kamakahelei of Kauai)
Pareah	Palea (Associate of Kalani'opu'u)
Tamataherei	Kamakahelei (paramount chief, matriarch of Kauai)
Taeòh	Ka'eo (husband of Kamakahelei)

Select bibliography

Editions of the Narrative

Samwell, David, *A Narrative of the Death of Captain James Cook, to which are added some particulars, concerning his life and character, and observations respecting the introduction of the venereal disease into the Sandwich Islands* (London: printed for G. G. J. and J. Robinson, 1786).
—— *Détails nouveaux et circonstanciés sur la mort du Capitaine Cook; traduits de l'Anglois* (Paris: Chez Née de la Rochelle, 1786).
—— *A Narrative of the Death of Captain Cook* (Honolulu: Hawaiian Historical Society, 1916).
—— *Captain Cook and Hawaii: A Narrative by David Samwell*. With an introduction by Sir Maurice Holmes (San Francisco: David Magee, 1957).

Works cited by the editors

Beaglehole, J. C., *The Journals of Captain James Cook* (Cambridge: Hakluyt Society, 1955–67).
—— *The Life of Captain James Cook* (Cambridge: Hakluyt Society, 1974).
Beddie, M. K., *Bibliography of Captain James Cook* (Sydney: [State] Library of New South Wales, 1970).
Borofsky, Robert, 'Cook, Lono, Obeyesekere, Sahlins', *Current Anthropology* 38 (1997), 255–82.
Bott, Elizabeth, *Tongan Society at the Time of Captain Cook's Visits* (Wellington: Polynesian Society, 1982).
Bowen, E. G., *David Samwell (Dafydd Ddu Feddyg) 1751–1798* (Caerdydd: Gwasg Prifysgol Cymru, 1974).
Colley, Linda, *Britons: Forging the Nation, 1707–1837* (New Haven: Yale University Press, 1992).
Constable, A. (ed.), *Letters of Anna Seward Written Between the Years 1784 and 1807* (Edinburgh: [unidentified publisher], 1811).

Cook, James and James King, *A Voyage to the Pacific Ocean, undertaken by the Command of His Majesty for making discoveries in the Northern Hemisphere* . . . (London: W. and A. Strahan for G. Nicol and T. Cadell, 1784).

D'Alleva, Anne, *Art of the Pacific* (London: Everyman, 1998).

Davies, W. Ll. 'David Samwell (1751–1798): Surgeon of the Discovery, London-Welshman and Poet', *Transactions of the Honourable Society of Cymmrodorion*, 1926–7, 70–133.

—— 'David Samwell: A Further Note', *Transactions of the Honourable Society of Cymmrodorion*, 1937–8, 257–9.

—— 'David Samwell's Poem – "The Padouca Hunt" ', *The National Library of Wales Journal*, II, 1941–2,142–52.

Dening, Greg, 'The Theatricality of Observing and Being Observed: Eighteenth-century Europe "discovers" the ? century "Pacific"', in S. B. Schwartz (ed.), *Implicit Understandings: Observing, Reporting and Reflecting on the Encounters between Europeans and Other Peoples in the Early Modern Era* (Cambridge: Cambridge University Press, 1994), pp. 451–82.

—— *Performances* (Melbourne: Melbourne University Press, 1996).

Fitzpatrick, Martin, 'The "cultivated understanding" and "chaotic genius" of David Samwell', in Geraint H. Jenkins (ed.), *A Rattleskull Genius: The Many Faces of Iolo Morganwg* (Cardiff: University of Wales Press, 2005), pp. 383–402.

Forster, George, *A Voyage Round the World*, eds N. Thomas and O. Berghof, (Honolulu: University of Hawai'i Press, 2000).

Gallagher, Robert E. (ed.), *Byron's Journal of Circumnavigation, 1764–66* (Cambridge: Hakluyt Society, 1964).

Gay, Peter, *The Enlightenment: An Interpretation: The Rise of Modern Paganism* (London: Weidenfeld & Nicolson, 1967).

Grant, Douglas (ed.), *The Poetical Works of Charles Churchill* (Oxford: Oxford University Press, 1956).

Hawkesworth, John, *An Account of the Voyages Undertaken by the order of His Present Majesty for making Discoveries in the Southern Hemisphere, and Successively Performed by Commodore Byron, Captain Wallis, Captain Carteret, and Captain Cook, in the Dolphin, Swallow and Endeavour* (London: Strahan and Cadell, 1773).

Jenkins, Geraint (ed.), *The Welsh Language before the Industrial Revolution* (Cardiff: University of Wales Press, 1997).

Johnson, Samuel, *A Dictionary of the English Language* . . . , 2 vols (London, seventh edition, 1783).

Adrienne L. Kaeppler, 'Tracing the History of Hawaiian Cook Voyage Artefacts in the Museum of Mankind', in T. C. Mitchell (ed.), *Captain Cook and the South Pacific* (London: British Museum Press, 1979), pp. 167–97.

King, James and Charles Ryskamp (eds), *The Letters and Prose Writings of William Cowper* (Oxford: Clarendon Press, 1981).

Kippis, Andrew, *A Narrative of the Voyages Round the World Performed by Captain James Cook With An Account Of His Life During the Previous and Intervening Period* (London: 1788).

—— *The Life of Captain James Cook* (London: Nicol and Robinson, 1788; London: Bickers and Son, 1893).

Kirch, Patrick V., and Marshall Sahlins, *Anahulu: The Anthropology of History in the Kingdom of Hawaii* (Chicago: University of Chicago Press, 1992).

Lamb, Jonathan, Vanessa Smith, and Nicholas Thomas (eds), *Exploration and Exchange* (Chicago: University of Chicago Press, 2000).

Leathart, William Davies, *The Origins and Progress of the Gwyneddigion Society of London* (London, 1831).

McMains, H. F., *The Death of Cromwell* (Lexington: University of Kentucky Press, 2000).

Morgan, Prys, *Iolo Morganwg* (Cardiff: University of Wales Press, 1975).

—— *The Eighteenth Century Renaissance* (Landybïe: Christopher Davies, 1981).

Namier, Sir Lewis and John Brooke, *The House of Commons 1754–1790* (London: HMSO, 1964), I.

Obeyesekere, Gananath, *The Apotheosis of Captain Cook* (Princeton: Princeton University Press, 1992).

O'Gorman, F., *Voter, Patrons and Parties: The Unreformed Electoral System of Hanoverian England 1734–1832* (Oxford: Oxford University Press, 1989).

Pearson, W. H., 'Hawkesworth's *Voyages*', in R. F. Brissenden (ed.) *Studies in the Eighteenth Century* (Canberra: Australian National University Press, 1973), pp. 239–57.

Porter, Roy, 'William Hunter: a Surgeon and a Gentleman', in W. F. Bynum and Roy Porter (eds), *William Hunter and the Eighteenth-Century Medical World* (Cambridge: Cambridge University Press, 1985), pp. 7–34.

Price, Richard, 'The Evidence for a Future Period of Improvement in the State of Mankind' (1787), in D. O. Thomas (ed.), *Richard Price: Political Writings* (Cambridge: Cambridge University Press, 1991), pp. 152–75.

—— 'A Discourse on the Love of our Country' (1789), in D. O. Thomas (ed.), *Richard Price: Political Writings* (Cambridge: Cambridge University Press, 1991), p. 195.

Sahlins, Marshall, *Historical Metaphors and Mythical Realities: Structure in the Early History of the Sandwich Islands Kingdom* (Ann Arbor: University of Michigan Press, 1981).

—— *Islands of History* (Chicago: University of Chicago Press, 1985).

—— *How 'Natives' Think, about Captain Cook for example* (Chicago: University of Chicago Press, 1995).

Salmond, Anne, *The Trial of the Cannibal Dog: Captain Cook in the South Seas* (London: Penguin, 2003).

Smith, Bernard, *European Vision and the South Pacific* (New Haven: Yale University Press, second edition, 1985).

—— *Imagining the Pacific* (New Haven: Yale University Press, 1992).

Spate, O. H. K., *The Pacific since Magellan*, vol. III, *Paradise Found and Lost* (London: Routledge, 1988).

Thomas, Nicholas, *Discoveries: The Voyages of Captain James Cook* (London: Penguin, 2003).

Wallis, Helen, *Carteret's Voyage Round the World, 1766–1769* (Cambridge: Hakluyt Society, 1965).

Williams, Glyn, *Voyages of Delusion: The Search for the Northwest Passage in the Age of Reason* (London: HarperCollins, 2002).

Williams, Gwyn A., *Madoc: The Making of a Myth* (London: Eyre and Methuen, 1979).

Zimmermann, Heinrich, *Zimmerman's Account of the Third Voyage of Captain Cook* (1781), trans. U. Tewsley (Wellington: Alexander Turnbull Library, 1926).

Index

Photographs, paintings and drawings are indicated by the page number followed by 'i'.